NATURE

AN ILLUSTRATED GUIDE TO COMMON PLANTS AND ANIMALS

BC

JAMES KAVANAGH

ILLUSTRATIONS BY RAYMOND LEUNG
LINDA DUNN , HORST H. KRAUSE
AND MARIANNE NAKASKA

Printed in Canada
First printed in 1993 5 4 3 2

The publisher: *Lone Pine Publishing*

10145-81 Avenue	202A, 1110 Seymour St.	1901 Raymond Ave. SW, Suite C
Edmonton, AB T6E 1W9	Vancouver, BC V6B 3N3	Renton, WA 98055
Canada	Canada	USA

CANADIAN CATALOGUING IN PUBLICATION DATA
Kavanagh, James, 1960—
Nature BC
Includes bibliographical references and index.
ISBN 1-55105-036-6

1. Zoology--British Columbia. 2. Animals--Identification. 3. Botany--British Columbia. 4. Plants--Identification. I. Krause, Horst, 1951- II. Title,
QH106.2B7K39 1993 574.9711 C931466-X

Introduction reprinted with permission of the author. Source: *Globe & Mail*, 2/7/87.
Natural Regions map reproduced with permission of Forestry Canada.
Viewing Areas map and text reproduced with permission of BC Ministry of Environment.

Cover and design: Beata Kurpinski
Editorial: Debby Shoctor, Glenn Rollans
Layout: Beata Kurpinski, B. Timothy Keith, David Baker
Maps: B. Timothy Keith
Printing: Quality Colour Press, Edmonton, Alberta, Canada

The publisher gratefully acknowledges the assistance of the Federal Department of Communications, Alberta Community Development and the Canada Council in the production of this book.

NATURE BC

CONTENTS

FOREWORD

This guide has been written in response to the need for a layman's guide to common species of plants and animals in British Columbia. Though there are already several field guides on the market which serve as identification guides to our local flora and fauna, many of these are overly complicated, and too detailed to be of use to the novice in the field.

Because this guide has been written for the novice, every effort has been made to simplify the presentation of the material. Descriptions, illustrations and distribution maps are grouped together for ease of reference, and technical terms have been held to a minimum throughout. A complete index of common and scientific names is included in the back as a further aid to finding information quickly.

I would like to acknowledge and express my grateful thanks to all who contributed to this guide. For their help in selecting species and guiding the initial layout and design of the book, thanks to the staff of the Royal British Columbia Museum, including R. Wayne Campbell (Birds), David Nagorsen (Mammals), Stan Orchard (Amphibians and Reptiles), Alex Peden (Fish), Philip Lambert (Invertebrates), and Richard Hebda (Botany). I am also deeply indebted to Gerald Straley of the University of British Columbia for his assistance in selecting the common trees, shrubs and wildflowers in the province, and to Dr. David Suzuki for allowing me to reprint his powerful essay on educating children about nature. For help with maps, thanks to Rick Thomas at the BC Ministry of Environment, Jocelyn Tomlinson at Forestry Canada, and the staff at BC Tourism's Vancouver office. Lastly, I would like to thank my two favourite mammals, Jill and Kristen, for their constant support and enthusiasm.

J.K.

To My Parents

HOW TO USE THIS BOOK

This book is a guide to the identification of 340 of the more common species of plants and animals found in British Columbia. Included are many familiar, widespread species and a few unusual ones which give our province its unique character. Most species are native to BC, though a few foreign species that are very common have also been included.

In order to make this guide useful in the field, the illustrations, text and distribution maps for each species are grouped together for ease of reference. In many instances, the illustrations alone may be sufficient for making a positive identification.

Illustrations – Many species show colour variations because of sex, age, time of year, and environment. For ease of reference, they have been illustrated in their most prevalent colouration. Animals, for example, usually feature the adult male in its breeding colouration.

Text – For each species, the text includes reference to its common and scientific names, average total length (animals) or height (plants) of mature organisms, habitat, key field marks, distinguishing behavioural characteristics, and items of general interest.

Distribution Maps – These maps, where available, indicate the **approximate** geographic range of species in BC. It should be noted that species are not evenly distributed within their range, and the reader should use the habitat description included in the text to better target the areas where they will be found.

In general, the species in each section have been arranged in evolutionary order, progressing from the least advanced to the more advanced families. Exceptions have been made in some cases to group different species according to superficial characteristics, in order to aid novices in field identification. The American Coot, for example, which belongs in the order of cranes and their allies (Gruiformes), has been grouped with ducks since it is duck-like in looks and habit, and is often found in the presence of ducks. Wildflowers have been arranged by colour, since research had shown this arrangement makes more obvious sense to amateurs than evolutionary ordering.

In order to compensate for any exceptions made to accepted scientific classification of species in the body of the book, the species checklists in the back of the book have been arranged in scientific order.

The best way to learn and recognize the plants and animals in BC is simply by practice. When you go on walks, get into the habit of carrying a field guide with you and noting the plants or animals you spot along the way. There are no tried and true methods of field identification, since each person's pattern of observation and learning is different. As you gain experience, you'll develop your own techniques for making quick and accurate observations. Don't be afraid to mark up the book and underline the characteristics that are most helpful to you.

As this is only an introductory guide, you'll likely want to supplement it at some point with more comprehensive information on your favourite area of interest. A list of references has been included at the back of the book to aid you in further study.

NATURAL REGIONS OF BC

The distribution of plants and animals throughout the province is largely determined by the climate, geography and soil conditions in each area. The conditions in each region dictate the kinds of vegetation it can support, and this, in turn, directly affects the distribution of animals.

BC can be generally divided into the following natural regions:

Boreal Forest

The boreal forest located in northernmost BC is a part of Canada's most dominant natural region. Characteristic plants include spruces, pines, firs, aspens, poplars, alders, grasses, mosses and lichens. Common animals include deer, moose, bears, wolves, foxes, hares, elk, grouse, owls, woodpeckers, jays and chickadees. This biome includes the quicksand-like "muskeg" areas of decaying vegetation which swallow up vehicles and travellers when thawed.

Subalpine

The subalpine region encompasses a transitional zone between the boreal forest and alpine regions. The vegetation at upper elevations is dominated by coniferous species including spruces, pines, firs and junipers. These are replaced by deciduous species at lower elevations including aspens, cottonwoods and birches. Alders, willows, Labrador Tea, bunchberry, paintbrushes and fireweed are common undergrowth species throughout much of the region.

Alpine Tundra

Characterized by cold weather, high winds and a short growing season, the alpine tundra is home to the hardiest species of plants and animals. Found on mountain slopes above the treeline, this biome supports an array of fast-growing plants including lichens, shrubs, herbs and mosses. Animal species which favour the area include mountain lions, grizzly bears, ptarmigans, pikas, birds of prey, caribou, mountain sheep and mountain goats.

Coast

This temperate rainforest environment is perhaps the country's richest ecological area. Buffeted by a mild climate and generous rainfall, it is home to a vast array of plant species including our largest trees; species of Douglas Fir and Sitka Spruce rise to over 90 m (300 ft.). Cedars, spruces, pines and fruit trees also occur in abundance. Representatives of most animal groups including fish, echinoderms and molluscs are common throughout this region.

Columbia

This region of middle elevation is dominated by coniferous species including spruces, hemlocks, cedars and larches. Nearer to the treeline, whitebark pine and alpine larch are common, as are a diversity of cold-resistant shrubs and wildflowers. Animals found in this region are similar to those found in the subalpine region.

INTRODUCTION

By Dr. David Suzuki

An internationally renowned geneticist and environmentalist, Dr. Suzuki has heightened our experience and understanding of nature over the years through numerous books, articles and television programs. In this poignant 1987 essay, he discusses the importance of allowing our children to appreciate nature on their own terms.

In spite of the vast expanse of wilderness in this country, most Canadian children grow up in urban settings. In other words, they live in a world conceived, shaped and dominated by other people. Even the farms located around cities and towns are carefully groomed and landscaped for human convenience. There's nothing wrong with that, of course, but in such an environment, it's very easy to lose any sense of connection with nature.

In city apartments and dwellings, the presence of cockroaches, fleas, ants, mosquitoes or houseflies is guaranteed to elicit the spraying of insecticides. Mice and rats are poisoned or trapped, while the gardeners wage a never-ending struggle with ragweed, dandelions, slugs and root-rot. We have a modern arsenal of chemical weapons to fight off these invaders and we use them lavishly.

We worry when kids roll in the mud or wade through a puddle because they'll get "dirty." Children learn attitudes and values very quickly and the lesson in cities is very clear – nature is an enemy, it's dirty, dangerous or a nuisance. So youngsters learn to distance themselves from nature and try to control it. I am astonished at the number of adults who loathe or are terrified by snakes, spiders, butterflies, worms, birds – the list seems endless.

If you reflect on the history of humankind, you realize that for 99 per cent of our species' existence on the planet, we were deeply embedded in and dependent on nature. When plants and animals were plentiful, we flourished. When famine and drought struck, our numbers fell accordingly. We remain every bit as dependent on nature today – we need plants to fix photons of energy into sugar molecules and to cleanse the air and replenish the oxygen. It is folly to forget our dependence on an intact ecosystem. But we do whenever we teach our offspring to fear or detest the natural world. The urban message kids get runs completely counter to what they are born with, a natural interest in other life forms. Just watch a child in a first encounter with a flower or ant – there is an instant interest and fascination. We condition them out of it.

The result is that when my seven-year-old daughter brings home new friends, they invariably recoil in fear or disgust when she tries to show them her favourite pets – three beautiful salamanders that her grandfather got for her in Vancouver. And when my three-year-old comes wandering in with her treasures – millipedes, spiders, slugs and sowbugs that she catches under rocks lining the front lawn – children and adults usually respond by saying "yuk."

I can't overemphasize the tragedy of that attitude. For, inherent in this view is the assumption that human beings are special and different and that we lie outside nature. Yet it is this belief that is creating many of our environmental problems today.

Does it matter whether we sense our place in nature so long as we have cities and technology? Yes, and for many reasons, not the least of which is that virtually all scientists were fascinated with nature as children and retained that curiosity throughout their lives. But a far more important reason is that if we retain a spiritual sense of connection with all other life-forms, it can't help but profoundly affect the way we act. Whenever my daughter sees a picture of an animal dead or dying, she asks me fearfully, "Daddy, are there any more?" At seven years, she already knows about extinction and it frightens her.

The yodel of a loon at sunset, the vast flocks of migrating waterfowl in the fall, the indomitable salmon returning thousands of kilometres — these images of nature have inspired us to create music, poetry and art. And when we struggle to retain a handful of California condors or whooping cranes, it's clearly not from a fear of ecological collapse, it's because there is something obscene and frightening about the disappearance of another species at our hands.

If children grow up understanding that we are animals, they will look at other species with a sense of fellowship and community. If they understand their ecological place — the biosphere — then when children see the great virgin forests of the Queen Charlotte islands being clearcut, they will feel physical pain, because they will understand that those trees are an extension of themselves.

When children who know their place in the ecosystem see factories spewing poison into the air, water and soil, they will feel ill because someone has violated their home. This is not mystical mumbo-jumbo. We have poisoned the life support systems that sustain all organisms because we have lost a sense of ecological place. Those of us who are parents have to realize the unspoken, negative lessons we are conveying to our children. Otherwise, they will continue to desecrate this planet as we have.

It's not easy to avoid giving these hidden lessons. I have struggled to cover my dismay and queasiness when Severn and Sarika come running in with a large wolf spider or when we've emerged from a ditch covered with leeches or when they have been stung accidentally by yellowjackets feeding on our leftovers. But that's nature. I believe efforts to teach our children to love and respect other life forms are priceless.

BC ANIMALS

BC is home to a vast array of animals which are adapted to exploit specific environments. The way in which different animals evolved from each other is illustrative of how species today are continuing to evolve.

Animals are living organisms which can generally be distinguished from plants in four ways:

1) they feed on plants and other animals;

2) they have a nervous system;

3) they can move freely, are not rooted; and

4) their cells do not have rigid walls or contain chlorophyll.

All animals are members of the animal kingdom, a group which comprises over a million species. Species are classified within the animal kingdom according to their evolutionary relationships to one another.

For the purposes of our simplified study, we have divided animals into two general groups — invertebrates and vertebrates.

Invertebrates

Invertebrates are animals which do not possess a backbone or an internal skeleton. Though not a bonafide scientific category like vertebrates, this designation is commonly used as a catch-all term for all other forms of animal life. Invertebrates in this guide are included in the section on shore life.

Vertebrates

Vertebrates are animals which have internal bony skeletons and a backbone composed of a series of vertebrae.

Vertebrates are divided into five categories:

1) Fishes

2) Amphibians

3) Reptiles

4) Birds

5) Mammals

The Fishes

The first fish-like creatures originated in the late Silurian period, about 400 million years ago. The group flourished during the Devonian period — also known as the Age of Fishes — and dominated the seas for the rest of the Palaeozoic era. Today, bony fishes are the dominant vertebrate group in existence, with more than 25,000 species worldwide.

The Amphibians

The first limbed land-dwellers, amphibians, evolved from fishes in the Devonian period about 340 million years ago. The major evolutionary advance amphibians made over their ancestors was their ability to breathe air and waddle about on land, thus freeing themselves from total dependence on an aquatic environment. With rich new habitats to exploit, amphibians quickly diversified and remained dominant on land for 100 million years.

In addition to the development of lungs and legs, amphibians also evolved a more efficient circulatory system than fish, having a heart with three chambers instead of two. Frogs and toads also developed external eardrums, an essential adaptation for surviving on land.

The Reptiles

Reptiles evolved from amphibian ancestors during the Carboniferous period, about 320 million years ago. Unlike amphibians, reptiles are completely terrestrial and can live independent of an aquatic environment. Young are nourished in shelled eggs until their birth and are hatched as miniature adults rather than going through a developmental (tadpole) stage. They are far more agile than amphibians on land, have dry, scaly skin which prevents water loss, and have a more efficient, four-chambered heart.

Because of their superior terrestrial adaptations, reptiles quickly took over as the dominant species on land. By the start of the Mesozoic period 225 million years ago, they dominated the land, sea and air and continued to rule the earth for the next 160 million years. At the end of this era, the group mysteriously underwent a mass extinction. The only groups that survive to the present day include turtles, snakes, lizards, crocodilians and tuatara (an iguana-like creature from New Zealand).

The Birds

Birds evolved from reptiles during the Jurassic period. Birds quickly became established as a group because of their ability to exploit a new habitat — the air. This new habitat provided them with a rich source of food and protection that was inaccessible to all other groups. Some of the key adaptations that allow them to fly include hollow bones, an enhanced breathing capacity and feathers (which some believe arose from reptilian scales).

Perhaps their greatest adaptation, however, is that birds are warm-blooded and able to regulate their own body temperature. Unlike all other species but mammals, they have the ability to maintain high activity levels during cold weather. A key behavioural adaptation is that they evolved complex communicative patterns and educate their young to a degree before they leave the nest.

The Mammals

Mammals evolved during the Jurassic and Triassic periods in the wake of the great reptilian expansion. Like birds, mammals are warm-blooded, and they likely succeeded as a group by inhabiting niches that did not appeal to the cold-blooded reptiles. As the reptiles died off, mammals quickly came to dominate the land, since they are very agile and can hunt prey easier and avoid predation better than reptiles or amphibians.

Grassland

The grassland is the warmest and driest part of the province. Grasses grow better in this area than trees because of the poor soil conditions and high winds. Rainfall is normally low, and the vegetation is primarily composed of drought resistant species including grasses and mat-forming shrubs. Shrubs and trees occur mostly in ravines and along waterways. Once the domain of the bison, this area supports numerous birds, ground-dwelling mammals, and many of the amphibians and reptiles found in BC.

Adapted from Forest Regions of Canada published by Forestry Canada, © 1992. Reprinted with permission of Forestry Canada.

Mammals evolved a unique reproductive strategy which was instrumental in their success. Unlike all other groups, the young develop in the female's uterus. After birth, they undergo an intensive nurturing by adults, acquiring behavioural lessons from their elders and siblings. As a group, mammals emphasize quality over quantity, producing far fewer young than other groups, but young with a much better chance of survival.

Geological Time Scale

Era	Period	Years Ago	Events
Cenozoic	Holocene	10,000	-dominance of man
	Quaternary	2.5 million	-first human civilizations
	Tertiary	65 million	-mammals, birds and insects dominate the land -angiosperms are the dominant land plant
Mesozoic	Cretaceous	135 million	-dinosaurs become extinct -mammals undergo great adaptive radiation -great expansion of angiosperms; gymnosperms decline
	Jurassic	190 million	-Age of Reptiles; dinosaurs abundant -first birds appear
	Triassic	225 million	-first dinosaurs and mammals appear -gymnosperms are the dominant land plant
Paleozoic	Permian	280 million	-great expansion of reptiles; amphibians decline -many marine invertebrates become extinct
	Carboniferous	340 Million	-Age of Amphibians -first reptiles appear -fish undergo great adaptive radiation
	Devonian	400 million	-Age of Fishes -first amphibians, insects and gymnosperms appear
	Silurian	430 million	-first jawed fish appear -plants move onto land
	Ordovician	500 million	-first vertebrates appear
	Cambrian	600 million	-marine invertebrates and algae abundant

MAMMALS

What is a mammal?

Mammals are warm-blooded animals that possess milk-producing mammary glands. Most are covered in hair (an adaptation which helps prevent loss of body heat to the environment), have four feet, a tail and several different kinds of teeth. Other physiological adaptations include a four-chambered heart, a diaphragm to increase breathing efficiency, and sweat glands. They also have three bones in the middle ear to enhance hearing (birds and reptiles have only one).

How to identify mammals

Mammals are secretive by nature and can be difficult to spot in the field. However, groups like rodents, rabbits, dogs, bears and big game species like elk and deer are commonly encountered if one knows where to look for them.

Since many mammals are wary of predators, some of the best places to look for them are in undisturbed areas affording some source of cover including woods and wood edges, swamps, thickets, rural fields and meadows.

When you spot a mammal, consider its size, shape and colour. Check for distinguishing field marks which can help you place it within its family. Consult the text descriptions to confirm your sighting.

Below are some examples of a few BC mammals. For more information see *Animal Tracks of Western Canada* by Joanne Barwise or *The Peterson Field Guide to Animal Tracks.*

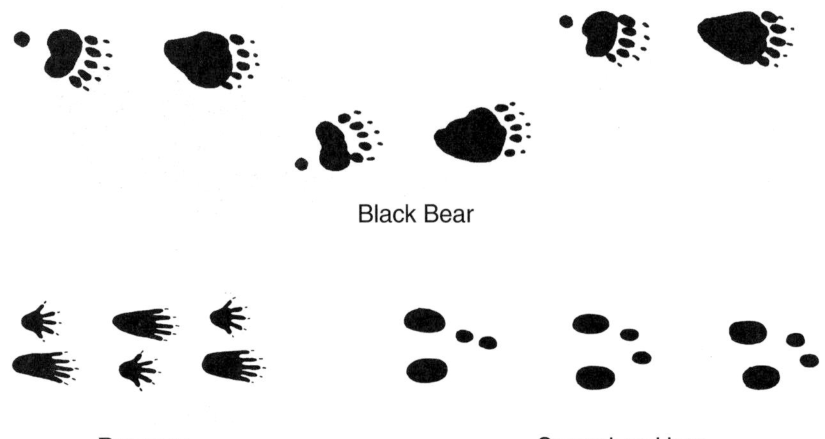

OPOSSUMS

Related to kangaroos and koala bears, the opossum is the only marsupial found in North America. The young are born prematurely and move to a fur-lined pouch (marsupium) where they complete their development attached to a teat.

VIRGINIA OPOSSUM

Didelphis virginiana
60-80 cm (24-30")

Found in woodlands in southern BC. Distinguished by its greyish fur, black-tipped ears and naked, rat-like tail. Opossums are most active in the evening and at night. They have the peculiar habit of pretending to be dead (playing "possum") when frightened.

INSECTIVORES

This group of insect-eating animals includes the moles and shrews. All have pointed snouts, sharp teeth and clawed feet.

MASKED SHREW

Sorex cinereus
10 cm (4")

A common insectivore found in moist habitats throughout the province. Distinguished by its brown coat, pointed nose and bead-like eyes. Highly active, it often eats more than three times its weight each day in insects. Their presence can often be detected by the small tunnels they make under leaf litter and vegetation. Nocturnal.

COAST MOLE

Scapanus orarius
15 cm (6")

Common throughout southwestern BC. Though rarely seen above ground, their presence can be detected by the numerous small mounds of earth they push up while digging their tunnels. Designed to dig, they have broad front feet which face outward, tiny eyes and no external ears. Active at day and night, feeding on earthworms and other small invertebrates.

BATS

The only true flying mammals, bats are common throughout BC. Most are furred, have large ears, small eyes and broad wings. Primarily nocturnal, they have developed a sophisticated sonar system — echolocation — to help them hunt at night. As they fly, they emit a series of high frequency sounds that bounce back off objects in their path. These waves reverberate back to the bat and tell it what objects or prey lie in its path. Diet consists of insects which they catch on the wing. During daylight, they seek refuge in caves, trees and attics. Bats are rarely harmful. They are valuable in helping to check insect populations.

LITTLE BROWN BAT

Myotis lucifugus
9 cm (3.5")

Found throughout the province in a variety of habitats from forests and fields to city parks. The most common bat in BC, it is identified by its small size and glossy coat which is dark brown above, buff below. Most active at dawn and dusk, it is sometimes spotted feeding during the day. Hibernates during winter.

BIG BROWN BAT

Eptesicus fuscus
12 cm (4.7")

Found in wooded and open areas throughout the province. Distinguished from the Little Brown Bat by its larger size and pale to dark brown coat. An erratic flier, it often hawks for insects near treetops or street lamps at dusk. It is the most common rabies carrier among bats.

PIKAS

Close relatives of rabbits, Pikas inhabit rock slides in the mountains. Active during the day, they can often be seen foraging for grasses and herbs.

ROCKY MOUNTAIN PIKA

Ocohotona princeps
19 cm (7.5")

Common near rock slides at high mountain elevations. Distinguished by its rounded body, large ears and lack of a tail. Active throughout the year, it spends the majority of the warmer months gathering food for winter. Pikas have the unusual habit of drying harvested vegetation in the sun (like hay) before storing it.

HARES AND RABBITS

Members of this distinctive group of mammals have long ears, large eyes and long hind legs. Primarily nocturnal, they commonly rest in protected areas like thickets during the day. When threatened, they thump their hind feet on the ground as an alarm signal. Hares and jack rabbits are distinguished from cottontails and rabbits in two ways: the former group are generally larger and give birth to precocial (active), rather than altricial (helpless) young.

SNOWSHOE HARE

Lepus americanus
45 cm (18")

Common in forests and brushy areas near swamps. Key field marks are its large hind feet and black-tipped ears. Its feet are heavily furred to allow travel over deep snow. Its coat is white in winter, brown in summer. It is most active at dawn and dusk.

NUTTALL'S COTTONTAIL

Sylvilagus nuttalli
36 cm (14")

Found in open forests and shrubby areas. The smallest rabbit-eared animal in the province, it is distinguished by its grey-brown coat, hairy hind feet and unmarked ears. Feeds primarily on grass. Most active at dawn and dusk, it rests in thickets during the day.

SQUIRRELS

This diverse family of hairy-tailed, large-eyed rodents includes chipmunks, tree squirrels, ground squirrels and marmots. All but the tree squirrels live in burrows on or under the ground throughout the year. Most are active during the day and easily observed in the field.

YELLOW PINE CHIPMUNK

Tamias amoenus
20 cm (8")

Common in coniferous forests. Distinguished by its small size, facial stripes and pronounced back stripes. It has expandable cheek pouches which are used to gather seeds and berries. Most hibernate in winter. Its call is a high pitched chipping. Its similar cousin, the Least Chipmunk (*Tamias minimus*) is the common chipmunk of northern BC.

RED SQUIRREL

Tamiasciurus hudsonicus
32 cm (12.5")

Abundant in coniferous and mixed woods, it also thrives in urban areas. Its coat is rusty red-black above, white below. Note the large, bushy tail. Calls include chatters, grunts and clicks. It spends the winter in ground burrows and tree nests the rest of the year. Feeds largely on conifer seeds it harvests throughout the year.

NORTHERN FLYING SQUIRREL

Glaucomys sabrinus
28 cm (11")

Found in mixed and coniferous forests, this is the only nocturnal squirrel in the province. Distinguished by its grey-brown coat, whitish underside and the loose skin between its front and hind legs. By stretching this loose skin taut, it can glide between trees for distances of up to 40 m (130 ft.).

HOARY MARMOT

Marmota caligata
70 cm (28")

Commonly found in alpine meadows near rock slides. A heavy-bodied rodent, it is told by its silvery fur, black feet and head, and shoulder patches. Lives in small colonies. Nicknamed "Whistler" for its shrill alarm call. Hibernates for up to eight months a year. Its less common cousins, the Yellow-bellied Marmot (*Marmota flaviventris*) and the Vancouver Island Marmot (*Marmota vancouverensis*) are also found in BC.

GROUND SQUIRRELS

These ground-dwelling rodents are widespread throughout southern and western BC. Strictly diurnal, they are easily observed feeding in open areas and running in and out of their multi-chambered tunnels. All have expandable cheek pouches to carry quantities of food to their burrows. When predators approach, individuals will sound warning calls causing all to flee to the safety of their burrows. Most populations are large and highly successful. All hibernate in winter. Their diet consists of seeds, insects and vegetation.

GOLDEN-MANTLED GROUND SQUIRREL

Spermophilus lateralis
25 cm (10")

This large, chipmunk-coloured squirrel is found in rocky areas in the mountain region. It is easily distinguished by its rusty head and long side stripes. Unlike chipmunks, it lacks facial stripes. A solitary mammal, it isn't above gathering in groups to accept handouts from hikers.

COLUMBIAN GROUND SQUIRREL

Spermophilus columbianus
36 cm (14")

Common in alpine grasslands and meadows, it is the largest ground squirrel found in the province. Identified at a glance by its grey back and rusty legs and belly. It hibernates seven to eight months of the year (August through March). These squirrels eat a higher proportion of meat and insects than other ground squirrels.

BEAVERS

A single representative of this family is found in abundance throughout BC. Families typically live in large, conical dams constructed from sticks and mud, though some river beavers live in bank dens.

BEAVER

Castor canadensis
71 cm (37")

This large rodent is found in wooded ponds, streams and lakes throughout BC. Key field marks are a glossy brown coat and large, flattened black tail. When threatened, it slaps its tail on the water as a warning signal. Beavers eat primarily bark and twigs, favouring aspen, birch and poplar trees. Largely nocturnal, it can often be seen skimming across the water at dusk.

MICE AND ALLIES

SOUTHERN BOREAL RED-BACKED VOLE

Clethrionomys gapperi
14 cm (5.5")

Common in damp woodlands with dense ground cover. Its coat is typically greyish-brown, with a wide, rusty band down the middle of the back. Grey phase also occurs which lacks a rusty back stripe. All have silvery bellies. It lives on the forest floor where it feeds on vegetation, seeds and berries. Active year-round, it can often be detected by the small tunnels it makes in the grass or snow. One of 10 vole species found in BC.

BOG LEMMING

Synaptomys borealis
13 cm (5")

Found in a variety of habitats throughout the province. Resembling fat mice, lemmings have long fur which gives them a rounded profile. Its coat is dark above, light below. Lemmings are an important food source year-round for many animals, including foxes.

HOUSE MOUSE

Mus musculus
13 cm (5")

This familiar mouse is very common near human dwellings throughout the province. It is identified by its grey coat, large eyes and ears and scaly tail. It normally lives in colonies. Females have up to 14 litters of 3-16 young annually. It feeds on grains, vegetables and refuse. Originally introduced from Europe, it is likely BC's most common rodent.

DEER MOUSE

Peromyscus maniculatus
17 cm (6.5")

Common and widespread throughout the province in a variety of habitats. It is distinguished by its bi-coloured coat, which is pale grey to reddish brown above and white below. Its hairy tail is also bi-coloured and nearly as long as the body. The young have grey coats. It feeds on seeds, buds, berries and insects. Active year round.

NORWAY RAT

Rattus norvegicus
30-45 cm (12-18")

Common near human dwellings throughout the southern part of the province. Distinguished by its large size, greyish-brown coat and scaly tail. Feeds on anything. Albino strains are commonly used in lab experiments. Its cousin the Black Rat (*Rattus rattus*) is also found in BC.

BUSHY-TAILED WOODRAT

Neotoma cinera
36 cm (14")

The only rat native to Canada, it is found in forests and along rocky alpine slopes. Distinguished by its large eyes and ears, long coat and bushy tail. It usually nests along cliffs, which it stains white and yellow with urine and faeces. Feeds primarily on vegetation and seeds. Also called a "packrat," it often hoards shiny objects.

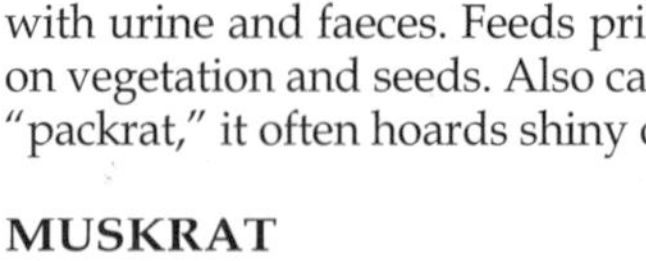

MUSKRAT

Ondatra zibethicus
56 cm (22")

This aquatic rodent is found in marshes, ponds and reedy lakes. The best field marks are its glossy brown coat, silvery belly and scaly, laterally flattened, black tail. Muskrats commonly live in conical, island-like lodges of vegetation, up to 1 m (3 ft.) above water. Highly active at dawn and dusk, muskrats feed on vegetation and small aquatic animals.

JUMPING MICE

WESTERN JUMPING MOUSE

Zapus princeps
23 cm (9")

Found near streams and marshes in moist meadows and open woodlands. Its coat is olive above, yellowish on the sides and white below. Identified by its large hind feet and long tail, which assist it in bounding across the ground, it is capable of leaping up to 2 m (6 ft.). Primarily nocturnal, it is also active during the day, but hibernates from October to May. One of three jumping mouse species found in BC.

PORCUPINES

Porcupines are dark, dog-sized creatures with coats of stiff, barbed quills.

PORCUPINE

Erithizon dorsatum
70 cm (28")

Common in forests and shrubby ravines throughout the province. Identified by its chunky profile, arched back and long, grey coat; its body is covered with barbed quills which protect it against most predators. When threatened, it faces away from its aggressor, erects its quills and lashes out with its heavily armed tail. The loosely rooted quills detach on contact and are extremely difficult to remove. Primarily nocturnal, its diet consists of leaves, twigs and bark. Sluggish on land, porcupines spend much of their time in trees.

WEASELS AND ALLIES

Members of this group usually have small heads, long necks, short legs and long bodies. All have prominent anal scent glands which are used for social and sexual communication. Primarily nocturnal, they feed largely on small mammals.

ERMINE

Mustela erminea
33 cm (13")

Also called the Short-tailed Weasel, it is found in open wooded areas and farmlands, usually near water. Field marks include its slender body, long neck and black-tipped short tail. Its summer coat is brown above, white below; winter coat is all white except for black tip on tail. A nocturnal hunter, it is a fearless, aggressive killer. Its larger cousin, the Long-tailed Weasel, looks similar in winter but has brown feet in summer.

MINK

Mustela vison
56 cm (22")

These nocturnal animals are common near water in a variety of habitats. Its rich brown coat and white chin patch are good field marks. Excellent swimmers, they are able to supplement their diet of small mammals with fish and frogs. In spite of recent efforts by environmentalists to protect these fur-bearers, in 1990-91 one million animals were trapped and farmed for their pelts.

STRIPED SKUNK

Mephitis mephitis
61 cm (24")

Common in open wooded areas throughout the province. Identified by its black coat, white forehead stripe and white side stripes. Protects itself by spraying aggressors with noxious smelling fluid from its anal glands, which it sprays up to 6 m (20 ft.). Feeds on vegetation, insects and small animals.

MARTEN

Martes americana
65 cm (26")

This largely tree-dwelling creature is found in remote coniferous forests. Its coat is yellow-brown to dark brown with a pale buff patch on the neck and chest. It feeds on squirrels, mice, birds and fish. Also referred to as Sable, its coat is highly valued by trappers.

BADGER

Taxidea taxus
76 cm (30")

Found in native grasslands and uncultivated pastures. A squat, heavy-bodied animal, it is identified by its long, yellow-grey coat, white forehead stripe and huge claws. A prodigious burrower, it feeds mostly on ground squirrels and other burrowing mammals. It is the only member of the weasel family to hibernate. Badgers are suffering a serious decline in population owing to a loss of habitat due to farming.

RIVER OTTER

Lutra canadensis
100-130 cm (40-50")

This sleek, water-dwelling mammal is found along stream and lake borders throughout BC. Identified by its long body, short legs and glossy, grey-brown coat. Hind feet are webbed. It feeds on crayfish, frogs and fish. This otter closely resembles the Sea Otter, which is found in coastal waters.

SEA LIONS

Sea lions are flippered mammals which belong to the family of seals with external ears. They are usually seen basking along shorelines.

NORTHERN SEA LION

Eumetopias jubatus
2.1-3.2 m (7-10.5 ft.)

Found along rocky shorelines in colonies. Opposite sexes look similar, though males are much larger than females. Yellow-brown in colour, these sea lions are practically hairless. Pups are dark brown. Their diet consists of fish and squid, occasionally stolen from fishermen.

RACCOONS

The Raccoon belongs to a family of mammals which includes the Coati of Central and South America and the Lesser Panda of Asia. Some experts also believe the Giant Panda belongs to this group.

RACCOON

Procyon lotor
89 cm (35")

Common in wooded areas near water in southern BC. Identified by its grey-brown coat, black mask and ringed tail. It feeds on small animals, insects, invertebrates and refuse, often dunking its food into water before eating. Primarily nocturnal, it may be abroad at any time.

DOG-LIKE MAMMALS

Members of this family have long snouts, large ears and resemble domestic dogs in looks and habit. Active year-round.

RED FOX

Vulpes vulpes
96 cm (38")

This sleek, large-eared animal is found in semi-open country throughout BC. Its coat is normally reddish, but black and red-black variants are not uncommon. The best field mark is its bushy, white-tipped tail. Primarily nocturnal, it feeds on small mammals, birds, berries and fruit.

COYOTE

Canis latrans
1.2 m (4 ft.)

Found in a variety of wooded and open areas throughout the province, it is identified by its yellow-grey coat, large ears, pointed nose and bushy, black-tipped tail. Holds its tail down when running. Largely a nocturnal hunter, it is often seen loping across fields at dawn and dusk. Feeds on rodents, rabbits, berries and carrion.

GRAY WOLF

Canis lupus
1.6 m (5.2 ft.)

Found in forested and tundra areas. Its coat is normally grey, but variants exist ranging from white to black. A species similar to the Coyote, the Gray Wolf is larger, has a broader nose pad and holds its tail high when running. Lives in groups with a complex social hierarchy. Feeds primarily on cloven-hoofed mammals.

CAT-LIKE MAMMALS

This group of highly-specialized carnivores are noted for their hunting ability. All have short faces, keen vision, powerful bodies and retractable claws. Most are nocturnal hunters.

CANADA LYNX

Lynx canadensis
1 m (3 ft.)

Found in heavily-wooded forests and swamps throughout BC. Distinguished by its long coat, tufted ears and short, black-tipped tail. Its large, thickly-furred feet are adapted for travelling over the snow. A nocturnal hunter, it feeds largely on Snowshoe Hare and some smaller mammals. Its rare cousin, the Bobcat, looks similar to the Lynx but has a tail which is black only on the upper side.

MOUNTAIN LION

Felis concolour
2 m (6.5 ft.)

Also referred to as the cougar or puma, it inhabits remote forests and swamps in the mountains and foothills. Field marks include its tan coat, whitish belly and long tail. A solitary hunter, it feeds largely on cloven-hoofed mammals, hares and other small mammals. BC is home to the world's largest number of Mountain Lions.

BEARS

This group includes the largest terrestrial carnivores in the world. All are heavy-bodied, large-headed animals, with short ears and small tails. Their sense of smell is keen, though eyesight is generally poor. Though BC's bears hibernate during winter, they are not considered true hibernators since they will often rise to go out of their dens during warm spells. Young are born in January-February.

BLACK BEAR

Ursus americanus
1.7 m (6 ft.)

The most common bear in BC, it is found in forested and swampy areas. Its coat is normally black, but cinnamon and blue-grey variants also occur. Note the straight snout profile. Its diet is 85 percent vegetarian and consists of berries, vegetation, fish, insects, mammals and refuse.

GRIZZLY BEAR

Ursus arctos
2 m (6.5 ft.)

Found in isolated mountain meadows and tundra areas, grizzlies normally inhabit higher terrain than black bears. The best field marks are its large shoulder hump and "dished" face. Its long fur coat has a frosted appearance. Primarily nocturnal, grizzlies feed on vegetation, fish, insects and large and small mammals, often caching uneaten game. Once common, grizzlies are currently regarded as a threatened species.

DEER AND ALLIES

This group includes many popular big game species including deer, moose and elk. Males of each species possess "true" antlers which are shed annually. Each year the antlers grow anew under a coating of "velvet" rich in blood vessels. When the antlers are fully grown — shortly before mating season — the velvet is shed. A few months after mating season the antlers are also shed.

MULE DEER

Odocoileus hemionus
2 m (6.5 ft.)

Found in open forests and wooded river valleys. Its coat is tan in summer, greyish in winter. Key field marks are the large ears and black-tipped tail. It feeds mostly on shrubs, twigs and grasses. Males shed their horns between January and March. Essentially a solitary species, mule deer often form herds during mating season and winter.

WHITE-TAILED DEER

Odocoileus viginianus
2 m (6.5 ft.)

Common in forests, farmlands and river valleys. Named for its large, white-edged tail which is held aloft, flag-like, when running. Its coat is tan in summer, greyish in winter. An agile, elusive deer, it can reach speeds of 65 kph (40 mph) and leap as high as 2.5 m (8 ft.). It is most active at dawn and dusk.

ELK

Cervus elaphus
2.4 m (8 ft.)

Also called Wapiti, the elk is common in open forests and meadows in the mountains and foothills. Distinguished by its large size, shaggy, dark neck and light rump. Most active at dawn and dusk, it feeds on grass, lichens and twigs. Elk usually travel in herds and are common near mountain townsites. Males shed antlers from February to April.

MOOSE

Alces alces
2.7 m (9 ft.)

Commonly found in swamp and forest areas in the mountains and foothills. The largest member of its family, the horse-sized moose is easily identified by its long, thin legs and overhanging snout. Males also possess enormous, flattened antlers and a prominent neck "bell" of skin and hair. Largely solitary animals, they are most active at dawn and dusk.

CARIBOU

Rangifer tarandus
1.2-2.2 m (4-7 ft.)

Caribou travel in herds on the tundra and in coniferous woodlands and muskegs. A thick-set deer with a whitish neck and huge, flattened antlers, this is the only group of the deer family in which males and females possess antlers. They undergo an annual fall migration from treeless expanses to timbered areas, travelling over 150 km per day on a set route.

SHEEP AND GOATS

Members of both sexes in this family possess un-branched horns which are never shed. Domestic cattle, sheep and goats also belong to this group.

BIGHORN SHEEP

Ovis canadensis
1.7 m (6 ft.)

Found in the mountains and foothills along rugged slopes and meadows. Stocky, grey-brown animals, they are easily identified by their huge, coiled horns. Powerful climbers, they have specialized "suction-cup" hooves which enhance their traction on the rocky slopes. Males and females form separate herds for most of the year.

DALL SHEEP

Ovis dalli
1.7 m (6 ft.)

Found in mountainous areas in northern BC above the treeline. Distinguished from the similar-looking Bighorn Sheep by its coat which may be white, black or grey. Usually herds in groups of six or more. In the fall, males battle each other in head-butting competitions to determine harem mastery.

MOUNTAIN GOAT

Oreamnos americanus
1.8 m (6 ft.)

Found high in the mountains on rocky slopes, usually above the treeline. Identified by its long, shaggy, white coat and pointed black horns. Its coat is shed in late summer. Like Bighorn Sheep, it possesses specialized hooves which enhance their traction on mountainsides. They are most active at dawn and dusk.

WHALES, DOLPHINS AND PORPOISES

Members of this group of mammals are strictly marine and never leave the water. Though fishlike in appearance, they breathe air through blowholes set high on their heads and have horizontal, rather than vertical, tail flukes.

PACIFIC WHITE-SIDED DOLPHIN

Lagenorhynchus oliquidens
To 2.7 m (9 ft.)

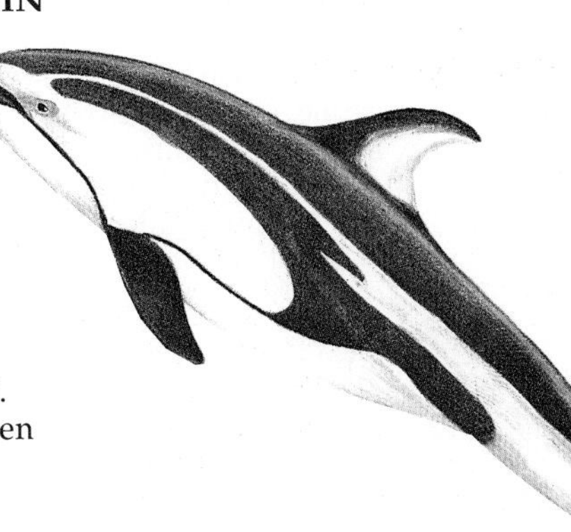

Frequently spotted near shorelines in winter and spring. Green-black in colour, it is identified by its pale side stripes and white belly. They travel in large groups of up to 1,000, feeding on small fish and squid. Their seasonal movements have been attributed to the availability of food.

DALL'S PORPOISE

Phocoenoides dalli
To 1.8 m (6 ft.)

Common in coastal waters, especially in winter. Easily distinguished by its black body and large, white ventral patch. Found in groups of two to 20 individuals, they often play around ships. Porpoises are generally distinguished from dolphins by their shorter snouts and stockier bodies.

KILLER WHALE

Orcinus orca
To 9 m (30 ft.)

Most abundant in spring and fall, particularly during salmon runs. Easily identified by its jet black body, white belly and white eye spots. Known as "sea wolves," Killer Whales have voracious appetites; the stomach of one individual was found to contain 13 porpoises and 14 seals. Considered the only natural predator of other large whales, they travel in "pods" of up to 40 individuals. Many are year-round residents.

GRAY WHALE

Eschrichtius robustus
To 14 m (46 ft.)

Seen in great numbers during migrations in winter and spring. Distinguished by their lack of dorsal fin and blotched, grey colour. Unlike the toothed Killer Whale, the Gray Whale feeds by straining small organisms from the water through huge, bony plates or "baleen" hanging from the roof of its mouth. Adults weigh up to 33,000 kg (37 tons).

HUMPBACK WHALE

Megaptera novaeangliae
To 15 m (50 ft.)

A common summer visitor to BC, it is distinguished by its humped back and scalloped flippers and flukes. A baleen whale, it feeds primarily on small crustaceans and fish it strains from the water. The most vocal of whales, its haunting calls can often be heard on the surface during calm days.

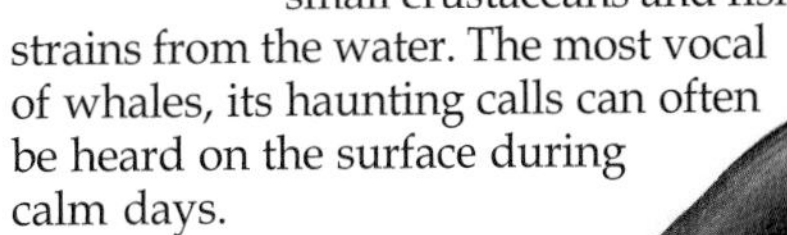

BIRDS

What is a bird?

Birds are warm-blooded, feathered animals with two wings and two legs. The majority can fly and those that cannot are believed to be descended from ancestors that did.

In addition to wings and feathers, birds are warm-blooded, have an efficient four-chambered heart and are insulated against the weather to enhance temperature regulation. They also have well-developed brains, keen senses and complex behavioural and communicative patterns. Adaptations for flight include hollow bones and an enhanced breathing capacity.

Like reptiles, birds are fertilized internally and lay eggs. Their eggs are different, however, and have hard, rather than leathery shells. The eggs are typically incubated by the male or female parent and the young are nurtured for a period before leaving the nest.

How to identify birds

As with other species, the best way to become good at identifying birds is simply by practice. The more birds you attempt to identify, the better you'll become at distinguishing species.

When you are out bird watching, the first thing you should note is the habitat you are exploring in order to know what kinds of birds to expect: ducks are found in marshes, herons on shorelines and woodpeckers in woods. You won't find a grouse on the water or a loon up a tree. When you spot a bird, try to determine its size and shape: is it small (sparrow), medium (crow), or large (heron)? Is it slender like a vireo, or chunky like a chickadee? Note the shape of its beak. Look at the colour and pattern of its feathers for any distinguishing markings. Does it have any unusual behavioural characteristics? Listen to its voice and try to distinguish a pattern in its song. When you've got a good mental picture of what it looks like, compare it to the illustrations. Consult the text to confirm your sighting.

If you are interested in becoming a serious birder, it is essential to become familiar with their songs. Bird song tapes are available from nature stores and libraries.

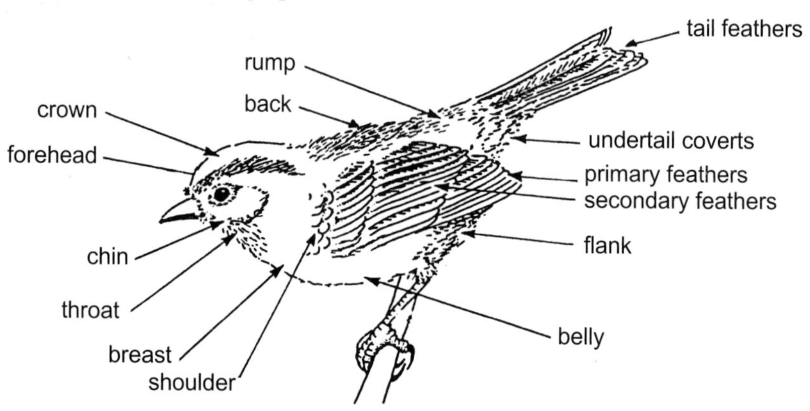

LOONS

These torpedo-shaped diving birds are commonly found on isolated stretches of water on lakes and large rivers. Excellent swimmers, they can dive to depths of 60 m (200 ft.). Loons have the ability to submerge their bodies at will and sometimes swim about with only their heads above water. Members of both sexes are similar.

COMMON LOON

Gavia immer
76 cm (30")

Found on wooded ponds and lakes, it is best known for its haunting call, which echoes at night. Distinguished in summer by its black head and black-and-white checkered back, its winter plumage is grey and white. Note the stout, straight bill. It feeds primarily on fish. The night call is a resonant "ha-oo, ha-oo-oo."

summer *winter*

GREBES

The members of this group of duck-like birds have short tails, slender necks and stiff, pointed bills (excluding the Pied-billed Grebe). Excellent divers, they have lobed toes rather than webbed feet and their legs are located near the back of the body to better propel them through the water. Weak fliers, they need to taxi across the water's surface before becoming airborne. Like loons, they are able to submerge their bodies at will. Noted for their elaborate, dancing, courtship rituals.

RED-NECKED GREBE

Podiceps grisegena
48 cm (19")

This grebe is common throughout BC. Distinguished in summer by its long, rusty neck, white cheeks and yellow bill. Non-breeding adults develop distinctive white crescents on their grey heads.

summer *winter*

WESTERN GREBE

Aechmophorus occidentalis
64 cm (25")

The largest grebe, it is found on large lakes and along the seashore. Distinguished by its long neck, slender bill and black-and-white plumage, these grebes winter along the coast in large numbers. They are noted for their spectacular courtship display where males and females dance across the water's surface in pairs.

HERONS

Large wading birds with long legs, long necks and slender bills. Most herons inhabit marshes and other shallows where they feed on fish, frogs and insects. Opposite sexes look similar. All fly with their necks folded into an "S" curve.

GREAT BLUE HERON

Ardea herodias
1 m (40")

A distinctive grey-blue bird found on the borders of rivers, streams and lakes. Distinguished by its large size, long legs, long, yellowish bill and whitish face. Note the black plumes extending back from the eye. It is often seen stalking fish and frogs in still waters from April to October.

CORMORANTS

Large, black, fish-eating birds with long, hooked bills, these birds often nest in colonies on rocky ledges. Unlike geese and ducks, cormorants do not have waterproof feathers and often perch with their wings spread-eagled to allow them to dry.

PELAGIC CORMORANT

Phalacrocorax pelagicus
70 cm (28")

Common in coastal waters, it is distinguished by its black, glossy plumage, slender neck and thin bill. At close range a dull red throat pouch is visible. Immature birds are all black. When swimming, they often point their bills upward at an angle.

SWANS

Swans are very large, white birds with long, slender necks. They fly with their necks extended in long lines or "V" formations. Opposite sexes look similar.

TRUMPETER SWAN

Olor buccinator
1.2 m (45")

Found on marshes, lakes and rivers. Its large size, white plumage and long neck are distinctive. It feeds on vegetation it pulls up by extending its neck underwater. These swans breed in northern BC. Its call is booming and trumpet-like.

GEESE

Geese are large, long-necked birds found near ponds and marshes. Highly terrestrial, they are often spotted grazing in fields and meadows. Their diet consists largely of grasses, grains and some aquatic plants. Noisy in flight, they are often heard before they're seen passing overhead.

CANADA GOOSE

Branta canadensis
60-100 cm (24-40")

Found near marshes, ponds, lakes and rivers throughout BC. The most common goose in North America, it is easily identified by its black head and neck, and prominent, white, cheek patch. Ten subspecies, which differ mainly in size, have been identified. Geese fly in a "V" formation when migrating. Pairs mate for life. Its call is a nasal "honk."

SNOW GOOSE

Chen caerulescens
70 cm (27")

A common migrant, it frequents marshes, sloughs and shallow lakes. Adults are typically white with black wing tips. Dark variants – often called Blue Geese – which have a white head and a dark blue body also exist. Note the distinctive bill shape. Young birds have greyish backs and white underparts. Flocks may number over 10,000.

DUCKS AND ALLIES

Smaller than geese, ducks have shorter necks and are primarily aquatic. Breeding males are generally more brightly-coloured than females, and both sexes have a brightly coloured band (speculum) on the trailing edge of the wing.

Ducks are divided into four groups: surface-feeding ducks that feed by tipping over and pulling up vegetation; diving ducks that dive beneath the surface for their food; fish-eating birds that have thin, toothed beaks for catching fish; and stiff-tailed ducks that are small, duck-billed birds that are almost helpless on land.

GREEN-WINGED TEAL

Anas crecca
36 cm (14")

The smallest duck in the province, it is found in shallow water lakes and ponds. The breeding male is identified by its brown head, glossy green face patch and vertical white wing bar. The female is distinguished from similar species by her short bill and unmarked forewing. The speculum is green.

female

male

BLUE-WINGED TEAL

Anas discors
38 cm (15")

A small duck often found in mixed flocks on marshes and ponds. The male is distinguished by its white facial crescent and white patch near its tail, while the female is a mottled brown colour. Both sexes have a blue wing patch and a green speculum.

female

male

AMERICAN WIGEON

Anas americana
50 cm (20")

Though primarily aquatic, these ducks can often be found nibbling grass on the shores of ponds and marshes. The male is brownish with white flanks, a white forehead and a glossy green face patch, while the female is distinguished by her bluish bill and flecked head. Speculum is green.

female

male

NORTHERN SHOVELER

Anas clypeata
50 cm (20")

Frequently found on ponds and sloughs. Its distinctive shovel-shaped bill is used to strain aquatic animals from the water. It also feeds on vegetation. The male has a green head, rusty sides and a blue wing patch, while the female is distinguished from other brown ducks by her large bill. Both sexes swim with their bills pointed downward. The green speculum is duller in the female.

MALLARD

Anas platyrhynchos
58 cm (23")

The ancestor of domestic ducks, the Mallard is abundant on ponds and marshes throughout the province. The male is identified by its green head, white collar and chestnut breast. The female is mottled brown. Both have a metallic blue speculum. Their call is a loud quack.

NORTHERN PINTAIL

Anas acuta
66 cm (26")

The most widespread duck in Canada, the Northern Pintail is found on shallow marshes and ponds. Distinguished at a glance by its long neck and pointed tail, the brown-headed male has a white breast and a white neck stripe. The female has a more pointed tail than similar species. Their glossy brown speculum is bordered in white.

DIVING DUCKS

BUFFLEHEAD

Bucephala albeola
36 cm (14")

A small, puffy-headed duck found on wooded ponds and rivers during nesting season. The male is distinguished by the large, white patch on its iridescent black head, while the female is grey-black and has a small, white, cheek patch. The Bufflehead is the only diving duck able to take off from the water without running along its surface.

male

female

HARLEQUIN DUCK

Histrionicus histrionicus
43 cm (17")

A small duck that summers on rivers and mountain streams and winters along the coast. The male's blue-grey plumage is unmistakable; the brownish female has three white facial spots and unmarked wings. They often float high in the water with cocked tails.

male

female

COMMON GOLDENEYE

Bucephala clangula
48 cm (19")

Found on wooded lakes and ponds during nesting season, they winter along the coast. The male is identified by its black and white body and the round, white spot between its eye and bill; the female has a brown head and an incomplete white neck ring. Their wings whistle loudly in flight.

male

female

WHITE-WINGED SCOTER

Melanitta deglandi
53 cm (21")

Plump, thick-necked birds found in flocks along the coast and on deep lakes and large rivers. The key field mark is a white wing patch on its dark body. Black males have a swollen bill and white eye patches; browner females have two light facial patches.

FISH-EATING DUCKS

COMMON MERGANSER

Mergus merganser
64 cm (25")

This large, fish-eating duck is commonly found on wooded lakes and rivers. Note the sleek "diving" profile and the long, slender bill. The male is identified by its iridescent black-green head and white underparts; the female has a crested rufous head and a sharply defined white throat.

STIFF-TAILED DUCKS

RUDDY DUCK

Oxyura jamaicensis
41 cm (16")

Found on ponds, lakes and sloughs, the Ruddy Duck is identified by its chunky body, white cheeks and uplifted tail. Males have prominent blue beaks during breeding season. Like loons, they can submerge their bodies at will and sometimes swim about with only their heads above water.

COOTS

Coots are chicken-billed birds often found in the company of ducks and geese.

AMERICAN COOT

Fulica americana
38 cm (15")

Common on fresh water in the summer and fresh and salt water in winter. The best field marks are its chicken-like white bill, white rear, long greenish legs and lobed toes. It feeds on the shore and in the water, and pumps its head back and forth when swimming. Seen April through September.

HAWKS, EAGLES AND ALLIES

Primarily carnivorous, these birds have sharp talons for grasping prey, and sharply hooked bills for tearing into flesh. Many soar on wind currents when hunting. Sexes are similar in most. A few groups of this order include: harriers — medium-sized, narrow-winged, low-flying hawks; hawks and eagles — medium to very large broad-winged soaring birds; ospreys — long-winged fish-eaters; and falcons — fast, narrow-tailed hunters with pointed wings.

NORTHERN HARRIER

Circus cyaneus
50 cm (20")

A slim, gliding hawk common to marshes and grasslands. The male is pale grey with a white rump; females and young are streaked brown. Long wings are tilted upward in flight. Unlike other hawks which scout prey from afar, it hunts by gliding close to the ground and surprising small animals and birds.

RED-TAILED HAWK

Buteo jamaicensis
56 cm (22")

This familiar hawk is often spotted gliding high over open fields and forests in search of prey. Identified in flight by its streaked breast, un-banded tail and whitish flight feathers; its red tail is usually an excellent field mark.

BALD EAGLE

Haliaeetus leucocephalus
90 cm (36")

Found along shorelines, its white head and brown body are unmistakable. Immature birds are mottled brown. The wings are held horizontal in flight. Its diet consists of fish, which it scoops from the water's surface or steals from other birds.

OSPREY

Pandion haliaetus
60 cm (24")

Found near water, it is distinguished by its white head and underparts and black eye patch. Wings are arched in flight unlike other large, soaring birds. It often hovers above the water's surface before diving for fish.

AMERICAN KESTREL

Falco sparverius
28 cm (11")

Formerly called the "Sparrow Hawk", this falcon is widespread in wooded and open areas throughout BC. Males are distinguished by their rusty back and tail, spotted blue wings and black facial marks. Its wings are long, narrow and pointed, and it pumps its tail when perching.

CHICKEN-LIKE BIRDS

These ground dwelling birds are chicken-like in both looks and habit. Most have stout bills, rounded wings and heavy bodies. Primarily terrestrial, they are capable of short bursts of flight. Males are usually more brightly coloured than females. Their diet consists of seeds, fruit and buds.

RUFFED GROUSE

Bonasa umbellus
43 cm (17")

A mottled brown bird found in open woodlands throughout BC. Key field marks include a crested head and black-banded, fan-shaped tail. Males can sometimes be heard during breeding season as they drum their wings loudly in the air. They usually winter in coniferous forests.

BLUE GROUSE

Dendragapus obscurus
45 cm (18")

Found in forests and thickets. The male is identified by its blue-grey plumage and yellow-orange patch above the eye; females and young are mottled brown. During territorial displays, the male produces huge "booming" sounds from his inflated, orange neck sacs.

WHITE-TAILED PTARMIGAN

Lagopus leucurus
30 cm (12")

Common in alpine meadows and open areas above the timberline. Identified in winter by its pure white plumage and black bill, it is brown in summer, with white belly and wings. The male has a red comb over his eye in spring. These birds prefer running to flying. They feed on seeds and insects.

RING-NECKED PHEASANT

Phasianus colchicus
76 cm (30")

Common in brushy margins of fields and forests. The male is identified by its shiny green head, red eye patch, white neck ring and very long tail, while the female is mottled brown with a long tail. They roost in trees or on the ground.

PLOVERS

These wading birds are distinguished from sandpipers by their thick necks, short bills and large eyes. Active feeders, they characteristically move about in short sprints. Opposite sexes look similar.

KILLDEER

Charadrius vociferus
25 cm (10")

As its Latin name indicates, the Killdeer is a highly vocal bird. Common in fields and pastures, it is distinguished by its brown back, white breast and two black neck bands, and its rump shows orange in flight. Its shrill call – "kill-dee, kill-dee" – is repeated continuously. When their nest is approached, adults will often feign injury to lure intruders away from the area.

SANDPIPERS

Sandpipers are long-legged wading birds normally found along shorelines. Most are brownish and have slender bills which they use to probe the sand and mud for invertebrates. Species are largely differentiated by size, bill length and tail, rump and wing patterns. Opposite sexes look similar in most species.

SPOTTED SANDPIPER

Actitis macularia
18 cm (7")

Probably the best known sandpiper in the province, it is found in a variety of habitats near water. A solitary bird, it is distinguished in the summer by its darkly-spotted, light underparts. It usually teeters back and forth on its legs when walking.

COMMON SNIPE

Capella gallinago
28 cm (11")

Found in marshes, bogs and grassy sloughs. Similar to the Long-billed Dowitcher, the Common Snipe is generally browner and has more pronounced streaking on its head and back. When flushed, it flies off in an erratic, evasive manner.

LONG-BILLED DOWITCHER

Limnodromus scolopaceus
29 cm (11.5")

A common migrant found in flocks in wet meadows and along lakeshores. Distinguished from most shorebirds by the length of its bill. Field marks include its rusty belly and dark breast bars. It feeds in shallow water and has a characteristic manner of repeatedly jabbing its bill in and out of the mud like a sewing machine. Its similar cousin, the Short-billed Dowitcher, is also found in the province.

LESSER YELLOWLEGS

Tringa flavipes
25 cm (10")

AND GREATER YELLOWLEGS

Tringa melanoleucus
36 cm (14")

Found near ponds, marshes and bogs. Some of the first shorebirds to arrive each spring, these grey-brown birds are the only tall, long-legged sandpipers with bright yellow legs. Note their white rumps. They can be distinguished from each other by their size and call: the Lesser has a one to three-note whistle; the Greater has a three to five-note whistle.

GULLS

These long-winged, web-footed birds are strong fliers and excellent swimmers. Adults are typically grey and white; immature birds are brownish. Most have square tails and are distinguished from each other by wing patterns and bill colour.

HERRING GULL

Larus argentatus
61 cm (24")

Found near bodies of water and garbage dumps. Distinguished by its grey back, white-spotted black wing tips and pink legs. Note the yellow eyes. Its varied diet includes carrion, garbage, eggs, young birds and aquatic animals.

GLAUCOUS-WINGED GULL

Larus glaucescens
65 cm (26")

A large, grey-mantled, white gull abundant in harbours, beaches and dumps. Its primaries are white near the tip, its eyes are brown, and its red bill spot blackens in winter.

BONAPARTE'S GULL

Larus philadelphia
33 cm (30")

A small gull found on coastal and interior waterways, it is common inland during breeding season. Primarily identified by its black head and bill and the flashy white wedge on its primaries, the winter adult is distinguished by its black bill, white head and dark spot behind the eye. It points its bill down in flight.

DOVES

These familiar birds are common and widespread throughout the province. All species coo. They feed largely on seeds, grain and insects.

ROCK DOVE (DOMESTIC PIGEON)

Columba livia
36 cm (14")

This introduced species is common in cities, towns and farmlands. Typically blue-grey in colour, several variants also exist which range in colour from white to brown. Key field marks include the white rump and black-banded tail.

OWLS

These square-shaped birds of prey have large heads, large eyes and hooked bills. Large flattened areas around each eye form "facial disks" which help to amplify sound toward external ear flaps. They are primarily nocturnal birds. Opposite sexes look similar.

GREAT HORNED OWL

Bubo virginianus
56 cm (22")

Found in forests and woodlands, this large, dark brown bird is distinguished by its large size and prominent ear tufts. Its plumage is heavily barred. Note its yellow eyes and white throat. It feeds on small mammals and birds and is sometimes spotted hunting during the day. Its voice is a deep "hoo-hoo-hooooo."

NORTHERN SAW-WHET OWL

Aegolius acadicus
18 cm (7")

This tiny owl inhabits marshes, meadows, evergreen forests and open country. It is distinguished by its small size, black bill and lack of ear tufts. Chiefly nocturnal, it feeds on insects and small mammals. Its call is a series of short whistles.

GOATSUCKERS

These nocturnal insect-eaters have large, swallow-like heads. Ancients believed that the birds sucked the milk of goats with their huge gaping mouths. Calls of most are distinctive.

COMMON NIGHTHAWK

Chordeiles minor
23 cm (9")

Found in open country and cities, these birds are spectacular fliers, and can often be seen hawking for insects during daylight. Identified by their long, pointed wings which extend beyond the tail when perching, white wing bars and white throat. They nest on flat-topped buildings in cities. Their call is a nasal "peenk."

HUMMINGBIRDS

The smallest birds, hummingbirds are named for the noise made by their wings during flight. All have long, needlelike bills and extensible tongues which are used to extract nectar from flowers. Their plumage is usually partially iridescent.

RUFOUS HUMMINGBIRD

Selasphorus rufus
9 cm (3.5")

This common migrant is found in meadows and forests with abundant flowering plants. The reddish back of the male is a key field mark; the female has a green back and reddish tail feathers. They winter in Mexico.

CALLIOPE HUMMINGBIRD

Stellula calliope
8 cm (3")

Found in coniferous woodlands and brushy meadows. The male's violet-streaked throat is a key field mark, while the female is green above, white below with a lightly-streaked throat. When defending their territory, males will often swoop down to "buzz" intruders.

KINGFISHERS

This group of solitary, broad-billed birds are renowned for their fishing expertise. Acrobatic feeders, they habitually plunge into the water from great heights. They are often found perched in trees bordering clear water.

BELTED KINGFISHER

Megaceryle alcyon
30 cm (12")

Found near wooded ponds, lakes and rivers throughout BC. It is identified by its large size, ragged head crest and long, broad bill. It often hovers over the water before diving after fish. Its call is a loud rattle.

WOODPECKERS

These strong-billed birds are usually spotted on tree trunks chipping away bark in search of insects. All have stiff tails which act like props as they forage. In spring, males drum on dead limbs and other resonant objects (e.g. garbage cans, drainpipes) to establish their territories.

DOWNY WOODPECKER

Picoides pubescens
15 cm (6")

A small, sparrow-sized, black-and-white woodpecker found in deciduous and mixed woods. The key field mark is its long, white, back stripe. The male has a prominent red patch on the back of its head. Its short, slender bill and small size help to distinguish it from the larger Hairy Woodpecker.

HAIRY WOODPECKER

Picoides villosus
23 cm (9")

Commonly found in deciduous forests and river groves. Similar to the Downy Woodpecker, it is distinguished by its larger size and longer bill. The female is similar to the male in both species but lacks the red head patch.

NORTHERN FLICKER

Colaptes auratus
30 cm (12")

Found in open woodlands, these robin-sized birds are the most common woodpeckers in the province. Key field marks include brown plumage, barred back and black bib. Its rump is white in flight. A newly designated species, it includes three formerly distinct species — the Yellow-shafted Flicker, Red-shafted Flicker and Gilded Flicker — which have been found to interbreed freely. Only the former two are found in BC. "Yellow-shafted" males are distinguished by their yellow wing linings, black "moustaches" and red head patches. "Red-shafted" males have reddish wing linings and red "moustaches." Females of both species are similar to males but lack "moustaches."

YELLOW-BELLIED SAPSUCKER

Sphyrapicus varius
to 20 cm (8")

Found in deciduous forests, groves and orchards. A mottled black and white bird, it is identified by its red forehead and long, white wing patch. Sapsuckers habitually drill orderly rows of holes in the trunks of deciduous trees and return periodically to feed on the sap and insects that collect in the holes.

FLYCATCHERS

These compact birds characteristically sit on exposed perches and dart out to catch passing insects. Many species have bristles at the base of their bills. Opposite sexes look similar.

OLIVE-SIDED FLYCATCHER

Nuttallornis borealis
18 cm (7")

Found in coniferous forests and mixed woodlands, often near water. Olive-grey above, it has a white throat and streaked breast. Note its large head and bill. When feeding, it habitually returns to the same perch. Its song is a loud, whistling, "quick three beers."

SAY'S PHOEBE

Sayornis saya
18 cm (7")

Common in open country, favouring dry, sunny locales. Identified by its rusty belly, pale back and black tail. Its call is a slurred "pheeeeur" or "pip-see-chee."

EASTERN KINGBIRD

Tyrannus tyrannus
20 cm (8")

This aggressive, noisy bird is found in open woodlands and shrubby meadows. Distinguished by its dark back, black mask, white underparts and the white band on the tip of its tail. Highly territorial, it will actively defend its nesting areas against all intruders, including man.

SWALLOWS

These streamlined, acrobatic fliers have short legs, short bills, long, pointed wings and long tails (often forked). Their wide mouths are adapted for scooping up insects on the wing. Often seen perched in groups along power lines and fences. Flight is undulating and graceful.

CLIFF SWALLOW

Petrochelidon pyrrhonota
15 cm (6")

Common throughout the province. Field marks include its white forehead, orange rump and square tail. It is often found near bridges and buildings, which are preferred nesting sites. Look for distinctive, jug-like nests constructed from mud pellets. Its song is a pleasant series of grating and creaking "cherrs."

TREE SWALLOW

Iridoprocne bicolour
15 cm (6")

Found throughout woodlands and open prairies, usually near water. It is identified by its blue-green back and white breast, and often glides in circles when airborne. Its song is a variable, three-noted, burbling twitter.

BARN SWALLOW

Hirundo rustica
18 cm (7")

This familiar swallow is found near farms and other rural habitations. Distinguished by its dark blue back, light underparts and rusty throat and forehead. Note the deeply forked tail. It often nests in building rafters. Its song is a cheery twittering.

CROWS AND ALLIES

These large, omnivorous birds are familiar to most. They generally have stout bills with bristles near the base. Opposite sexes look similar.

GRAY JAY

Perisoreus canadensis
28 cm (11")

Also known as the Canada Jay or Whiskey Jack, it is common in coniferous forests. Distinguished by its fluffy grey plumage, white face and dark neck patch. One of the tamest birds in the province, it will often approach campers for food scraps, but feeds largely on conifer seeds.

STELLAR'S JAY

Cyanocitta stelleri
30 cm (12")

Common in coniferous forests, it is the only crested jay in BC. Its plumage is sooty below and blue-grey above, while the white eyebrow, forehead and chin patches vary. Like the Gray Jay, it will often frequent campsites and human dwellings in search of handouts.

AMERICAN CROW

Corvus brachyrhynchos
48 cm (19")

Very common in a variety of habitats throughout the province. A familiar sight in rural areas, it is identified by its black plumage and thick, black bill. A dedicated omnivore, it eats everything from insects and grain to small birds and refuse. Its call is a distinct "caw."

COMMON RAVEN

Corvus corax
64 cm (25")

Common in wilderness and open country throughout the foothills and northern reaches of the province. Similar to the crow, it is distinguished by its larger size, heavier beak, keeled tail and low, croaking call. Primarily a scavenger, it is often found near dumps and refuse sites.

BLACK-BILLED MAGPIE

Pica pica
76 cm (30")

Found near fields, pastures, thickets and roadsides throughout the province. Distinguished by its black hood, long, wedge-shaped tail and white wing patches. Often seen scavenging in fields and along roadsides. Feeds primarily on small mammals and insects.

CHICKADEES

These small, plump birds have large heads, small bills and fluffy plumage. Their diet consists of seeds, berries and insects. Opposite sexes look similar.

BLACK-CAPPED CHICKADEE

Parus atricapillus
13 cm (5")

Common in forests and semi-wooded areas. Identified by its small size, fluffy grey plumage, black cap and chin and white face patch. Abundant in cities and towns during winter, it is easily attracted to feeders. Its voice is a clear "chick-a-dee-dee-dee."

BOREAL CHICKADEE

Parus hudsoniscus
13 cm (5")

Found primarily in dense coniferous forests. Distinguished by its brown head and back, rusty sides and white cheeks. Its voice is a blurry, slow, "chick-a-day-day."

NUTHATCHES

Nuthatches are stout little birds with thin, sharp bills and stumpy tails. They are usually spotted clambering about on tree trunks and branches, often upside-down.

RED-BREASTED NUTHATCH

Sitta canadensis
13 cm (5")

Found in coniferous and mixed wood forests, this chunky little bird creeps about on tree trunks and branches searching for insects beneath the bark, habitually descending trunks head first. Key field marks are its black-and-white eye stripes and short tail. Its call is a nasal "hee-hee-hee-hee."

WRENS

These little brown birds have the distinctive habit of cocking their tails in the air. They spend much of their time on the ground foraging for insects.

HOUSE WREN

Troglodytes aedon
13 cm (5")

Found in thickets and wooded areas near farmlands and towns, it is distinguished by its barred and cocked tail and slender bill. An aggressive little bird, it moves about in quick, jerky motions, often scolding intruders. Its song is a gurgling melody.

THRUSHES

This group of woodland birds includes many good singers. Most feed on the ground. Opposite sexes look similar.

MOUNTAIN BLUEBIRD

Sialia currucoides
18 cm (7")

Found in semi-open woodlands at higher elevations. The male's turquoise plumage is unmistakable. The tawny female shows turquoise on the wings, especially in flight. It typically hovers over the ground when searching for insects. Its song is a warbling whistle.

AMERICAN ROBIN

Turdus migratorius
25 cm (10")

Very common in towns, fields and open woodlands. A familiar bird to most, it is identified by its grey back and rusty breast. It usually forages on the ground for insects, snails and worms. Males begin their liquid singing as early as March.

VARIED THRUSH

Ixoreus naevius
25 cm (10")

Common in coniferous woodlands. Similar to the robin in looks and habits, it is distinguished by its black eye stripe, orange wing bars and dark breast band. It feeds on the ground. Its song is an unmelodious series of buzzes and whistles.

KINGLETS

A family of tiny active birds with small bills, which feed primarily on insects.

RUBY-CROWNED KINGLET

Regulus calendula
10 cm (4")

Found in mixed and coniferous forests, this tiny, green bird is distinguished by its short tail, broken eye ring and two white wing patches. It habitually flicks its wings nervously while perching. The male's red cap is often difficult to spot. Its song is comprised of three to four notes in variable combinations, e.g.: "see, see, see, too, too, too, tee-do-da-dee."

WAXWINGS

This group of gregarious birds are named for their red wing marks which look like waxy droplets. Told at a glance by their sleek, crested heads and yellow-tipped tails.

CEDAR WAXWING

Bombycilla cedrorum
18 cm (7")

Commonly found in open, deciduous woods, it is identified by its crested head, yellowish abdomen and yellow-tipped tail. The undertail coverts (where the tail connects with the body) are white. Its diet consists largely of berries and insects.

BOHEMIAN WAXWING

Bombycilla garrulus
20 cm (8")

Found in coniferous and mixed forests during the summer. It is distinguished from the Cedar Waxwing by its grey belly, white wing patches and rusty undertail coverts. Large flocks often travel into suburban areas during winter to feast on the berries of ornamental trees and shrubs. If the berries have fermented, the birds become inebriated and unable to fly.

STARLINGS

The Crested Mynah also occurs in BC.

EUROPEAN STARLING

Sturnus vulgaris
23 cm (9")

This introduced species is found in a variety of habitats throughout the province. Similar to a blackbird, it is distinguished by its chubby profile and short tail. Its bill is yellowish at certain times of the year. Considered a pest by many, the Starling is an aggressive bird that competes with native species for food and nesting sites. It usually travels in huge flocks.

VIREOS

Vireos are small, greenish birds with hooked bills which are more often heard than seen. They build fragile, cup-like nests in the forks of tree limbs.

RED-EYED VIREO

Vireo olivaceus
15 cm (6")

A small, greenish bird found in deciduous and mixed forests. Distinguished by its grey cap and black-banded, white eye stripe, the red eye is a poor field mark. This vireo inhabits rural and urban areas. Its song is a monotonous repetition of small phrases which rise and fall.

WOOD WARBLERS AND ALLIES

Members of this large family of highly active, insect-eating birds are distinguished from other small birds by their thin, pointed bills. Most species display some yellow or green. Males tend to be more brightly coloured than females and are the only singers. Species are distinguished by head markings and presence or absence of wing bars.

YELLOW WARBLER

Dendroica petechia
13 cm (5")

Common near shrubs and thickets in river valleys, coulees and urban areas. A bright yellow warbler, it is distinguished by its yellow-spotted tail. Males also have rusty streaks on their breast. Its song is a cheery "sweet, sweet, sweet."

YELLOW-RUMPED WARBLER

Dendroica coronata
15 cm (6")

Common in coniferous forests, the bluish male is identified by its black breast, yellow cap and yellow rump. A newly designated species, it includes two formerly distinct species — the Myrtle Warbler and Audubon's Warbler — which have since been found to interbreed freely. The "Myrtle" male has a white throat, while the "Audubon" male has a yellow throat and thick white wing patch. Brownish females have markings similar to males on their throats and rumps.

ORANGE-CROWNED WARBLER

Vermivora peregrina
13 cm (5")

Common in open, brushy woodlands, it is best described as a nondescript, yellow-green bird with faint flank stripes. Its crown patch is rarely visible. Its song is a chippy trill of 18 or more notes.

AMERICAN REDSTART

Setophaga ruticilla
15 cm (6")

An active, insectivorous bird common in deciduous and mixed woods. The distinctive black male has bright orange wing and tail patches; females are olive-coloured with yellowish wing and tail patches. Its song is a clear "zee-zee-zee-zee-ZEE," or "teetza-teetza-teetza-teetza."

NORTHERN WATERTHRUSH

Sieurus noveboracensis
15 cm (6")

Common near bogs and marshes, It is identified by its greenish colour and heavily streaked breast. Feeds on the ground and teeters when it walks, like the Spotted Sandpiper. Note the light eye stripe. Its song is a repetitive chattering of identical phrases followed by a sharp "chink."

WEAVER FINCHES

A single member of this Old World family occurs in BC.

HOUSE SPARROW

Passer domesticus
15 cm (6")

Very common throughout the province in a variety of habitats. The black throat and brown nape of the male are diagnostic; females and young are dull brown with a light eye stripe. These birds gather in large flocks when not breeding.

BLACKBIRDS AND ALLIES

A diverse group of birds ranging from iridescent black birds to brightly coloured tanagers and orioles. All have conical, sharp-pointed bills.

BROWN-HEADED COWBIRD

Molothrus ater
18 cm (7")

Common on farmlands and fields, they are often spotted feeding near domestic livestock. The male is distinguished by its brown head and finch-like bill, while the grey female is noted for her parasitic habit of laying eggs in the nests of other birds. While some species remove the new egg, most will raise the orphaned cowbird as their own.

BREWER'S BLACKBIRD

Euphagus cyanocephalus
23 cm (9")

Common in fields and pastures in southeastern B.C. Key field marks are its iridescent, purple head and green-black body. It often perches in large groups along fences and wires. Forages on the ground for grain and insects.

RED-WINGED BLACKBIRD

Agelaius phoeniceus
25 cm (10")

Found in sloughs, marshes and wet fields, it usually nests in reeds or tall grass near water. Black males have distinctive red shoulder patches; brown females are heavily streaked and lack shoulder patches. Found in large flocks.

WESTERN MEADOWLARK

Sturnella neglecta
18 cm (7")

Common in grassy fields, meadows and marshes, the key field marks are its long bill, bright yellow breast, white-edged tail and the dark, V-shaped neckband. Its flute-like, gurgling song is also distinctive.

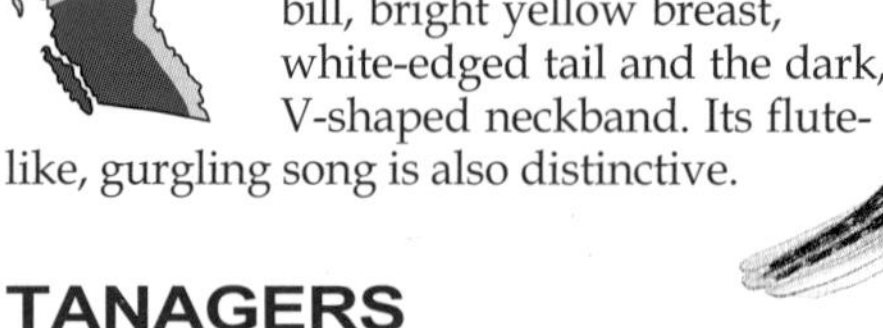

TANAGERS

Tanagers are colourful forest birds with slender, swollen bills.

WESTERN TANAGER

Piranga ludoviciana
18 cm (7")

Fairly common in coniferous and mixed forests. The male is easily identified by its red head, yellow body and black wings; note the notched tail. Females and young are olive-coloured with two light wing bars. Its song is similar to a Robin's.

FINCHES

Members of this family are brightly coloured and have short, thick, seed-cracking bills.

AMERICAN GOLDFINCH

Carduelis tristis
13 cm (5")

One of the last birds to arrive in the spring, they are often found in wooded groves and bushy areas. The male is bright yellow with a black cap, tail, wings and a white rump, while the olive-coloured female is similarly marked, but lacks a cap. Often found in flocks, it can be identified on the wing by its deeply undulating flight. Its canary-like song is bright and cheery.

PINE SISKIN

Carduelis pinus
13 cm (5")

Common in coniferous and mixed forests, these birds are easily attracted to feeders. Identified by their heavily streaked plumage and notched tail, the small yellow patches on its wings and tail are most prominent in flight. It is often found flocking in the tops of trees.

RED CROSSBILL

Loxia curvirostra
15 cm (6")

Found in forests, fields and swamps. Identified by its brick-red body, dark wings and dark tail, its bill is crossed near the tip, though this is often hard to discern in the field. It feeds primarily on conifer seeds in parrot-like fashion.

EVENING GROSBEAK

Coccothraustes vespertinus
18 cm (7")

Found in coniferous forests. The male is distinguished by its large size, yellow plumage, huge beak and white wing patches, while the female has a dull yellow back and breast and dingier wing patches. Often frequenting feeders, they are especially attracted to sunflower seeds and salt. Their flight is undulating.

SPARROWS

Sparrows are small, brownish birds with stout, seed-cracking bills. Species are distinguished from one another by head and breast markings, tail shape and habitat.

CHIPPING SPARROW

Spizella passerina
13 cm (5")

Common near open forests, fields and lawns. Distinguished by its red cap, white eyebrow line, the black line through its eye and unstreaked breast. Its nests are often victimized by Brown-headed Cowbirds. Its song is a repetitive, sharp, "chip."

SONG SPARROW

Melospiza melodia
15 cm (6")

Very common in bushes and woodlands near water. Identified by its long tail and dark breast spot, it often "pumps" its tail in flight. It often visits feeders and birdbaths, and also forages along the ground. Its melodious song usually begins with three or four similar notes.

FOX SPARROW

Passerella iliaca
15 cm (6")

Common in thickets and dense, brushy areas. It is identified by its brown streaked underparts and central breast spot. It scratches noisily along the ground when foraging, and also visits feeders and birdbaths. Its song is a loud, whistling melody: "hear, hear, sweet, sweet, sweetly."

DARK-EYED JUNCO

Junco hyemalis
15 cm (6")

Found in brushy fields and meadows bordering coniferous and mixed forests. Key field marks are its dark head, whitish bill, white belly and white-edged tail. A newly designated species, it includes four formerly distinct species – the Slate-coloured Junco, Oregon Junco, Gray-headed Junco and White-winged Junco – which have been observed to interbreed freely where their ranges overlap. Of these, only the first two occur in BC. The slate-coloured version has grey sides and a grey back. The Oregon version has a black head and a brown back.

REPTILES

What is a reptile?

Reptiles are fully terrestrial, cold-blooded vertebrates. Most lay eggs. They are represented in BC by two groups:

1. Turtles;

2. Lizards and snakes.

The greatest advance reptiles made over their amphibian ancestors was the evolution of the amniotic egg. The shelled egg allows the embryo to develop in a watery medium which is protected from drying out. The yolk sac attached to the embryo provides food and the young hatch fully developed, rather than having to go through a larval stage.

Reptiles have several other characteristics which make them better suited for life on land than amphibians. Their respiratory and circulatory systems are more advanced and enhance the oxygen content of the blood being circulated through the system. They have scaly, dry skin which prevents water loss and protects them from enemies. Reptiles are also better able to defend themselves, having sharp teeth or beaks capable of inflicting wounds.

How to identify reptiles

Turtles often sun themselves on rocks and logs near water. They are wary and should be approached cautiously.

The best time to look for snakes is in the early morning or late afternoon when it's not too hot. Look in meadows, fields, woods, or on the margins of ponds, checking under sun-warmed logs and rocks where they may be resting. The gopher snake and rattlesnake often sun themselves in open areas.

Since there are relatively few species of reptiles in the province, field identification for all but the garter snakes (whose stripe colours may vary) is simple. If you decide to handle garter snakes, be warned that they will often bite when provoked.

TURTLES

Turtles are easily distinguished by their large, bony shells. The shell is formed from widened ribs and serves to protect the turtle from most predators. Like all reptiles, turtles are air breathers and possess lungs; however, they are also able to breathe underwater from gill-like respiratory surfaces on their mouth and anus. They are most active in spring during mating season. Females lay their eggs in holes excavated in soft soil near water. The young hatch either in late summer or the following spring and are independent from birth. Most are omnivores and eat a wide variety of plant and animal matter.

PAINTED TURTLE

Chrysemys picta
to 25 cm (10")

Found in ponds, quiet streams, marshes and ditches in southern BC. Distinguished by its smooth, greenish shell marked by an irregular pattern of yellow lines. It is often spotted basking in the sun on partially submerged rocks or logs. It feeds on vegetation, crustaceans and insects. Easily tamed, it is often sold in pet shops.

LIZARDS

Lizards are scaly-skinned creatures which usually have moveable eyelids, visible ear openings, claws and toothed jaws. Most lay eggs, though in some species the females retain the eggs in their bodies and give birth to live young. Highly terrestrial, lizards are well adapted for travel on land and have a more upright stance than amphibians. Fond of moist, hot climates, they have yet to penetrate far into Canada.

WESTERN SKINK

Eumeces skiltonianus
8 cm (3")

Found in woodlands and forests under ground litter. Identified by its cylindrical, lizard-like body and a broad, dorsal stripe edged in black. It is most active in the late afternoon. Like many lizards, its tail readily detaches when grasped by a predator; in such instances the detached tail wiggles, providing a diversion which often allows the tailless skink to escape. The tail grows back over a few weeks.

NORTHERN ALLIGATOR LIZARD
Gerrhonotus coeruleus
28 cm (11")

Found under ground litter in cool, moist woodlands. Distinguished by its elongated, stiff body, with a distinctive fold along either side, and long tail. It is greenish above; light below. Active during the day, it feeds largely on insects and snails. Its tail is readily lost.

SNAKES

Snakes are limbless reptiles with moist, scaly skin, toothed jaws, no ear openings or eyelids and a single row of belly scales. They move by contracting their muscles in waves and undulating over the ground. All are carnivorous and swallow their prey whole. They flick their tongues in and out constantly to "taste" and "smell" the air around them. Most continue to grow in length during their life and shed their outer skin periodically. Only the Prairie Rattlesnake is considered dangerous to man.

COMMON GARTER SNAKE
Thamnophis sirtalis
to 1.2 m (47")

This dark snake is commonly found near water in meadows, farmlands and valleys, and is the most common snake in North America. It is distinguished in the field by the red or orange bars between its yellow dorsal stripe and yellow side stripes. This snake is a good swimmer.

WANDERING GARTER SNAKE
Thamnophis elegans
to 1.7 m (67")

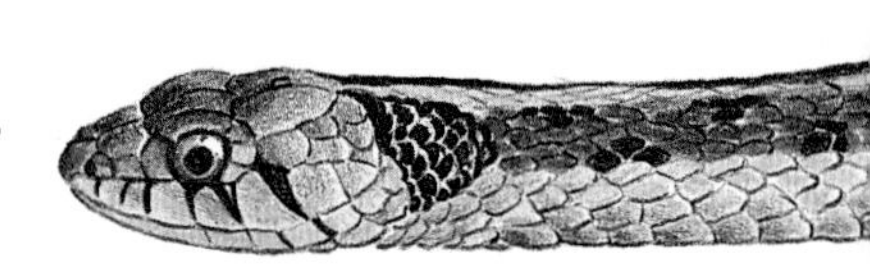

Found in both terrestrial and aquatic habitats in southern BC. The yellow-orange dorsal stripe extends the length of its body. It is identified by its checkerboard pattern of dark marks between its back and side stripes. It often enters the water to feed or escape predation, but may be seen basking in open areas early in the day.

NORTHWESTERN GARTER SNAKE

Thamnophis ordinoides
to 70 cm (27")

Found in moist forests, meadows and pastures. A small snake with a broad, yellow-red dorsal stripe, faint side stripes and a yellowish belly. It may sometines be intirely black. It feeds on slugs,salamanders, worms and frogs.

GOPHER SNAKE

Pituophis melanoleucus
to 2.5 m (98")

Found on farmland and prairies in southern BC. Distinguished by its large size, light colour and dark blotches on its back and sides. Though non-poisonous, it imitates a rattlesnake when threatened by coiling up, hissing loudly, vibrating its tail and striking out at its aggressor. Eats primarily small rodents and is valued for pest control on farms. It is also capable of climbing trees to raid bird nests.

PRAIRIE RATTLESNAKE

Crotalus viridis
to 1.3 m (51")

Found in variable habitats from river valleys and prairies to mountain forests at 3,350 m (11,000 ft.). A darkly blotched, greenish-brown snake, it is best identified by its tail rattle, which it vibrates when threatened. Note the flattened head and defined neck. A pit viper, it has heat-sensing areas between its eye and nostril which help it to detect prey. Enlarged front fangs have hollow canals which inject poison into prey when it strikes. It eats mostly rodents. Large numbers often overwinter in common dens.

AMPHIBIANS

What is an amphibian?

Amphibians are smooth-skinned, cold-blooded vertebrates which live in moist habitats. They are able to breathe through lungs, skin, gills or a combination of all three. The two distinct groups of amphibians found in BC are:

1. Salamanders;
2. Frogs and toads.

Like reptiles, amphibians are cold-blooded and are unable to maintain a constant body temperature. Their activity levels are therefore largely determined by their environment, being enhanced in warm weather and reduced in cold.

While amphibians live much of their lives on land, they still depend on a watery environment to complete their life cycle. Most reproduce by laying eggs in or near the water. The young hatch as swimming larvae, or tadpoles, which breathe by means of gills. After a short developmental period, the larvae metamorphose into young adults with lungs and legs.

How to identify amphibians

Of the amphibians, the frogs and toads are probably the easiest to observe since they loudly announce their presence to all within earshot during breeding season. Salamanders are far more secretive and rarely venture out of their cool, moist habitats.

The best time to look for frogs and toads is just after dark when they are most vocal. If you approach the water quietly with an artificial light, you should be able to get fairly close.

SALAMANDERS

Salamanders are tailed, lizard-like creatures that inhabit moist areas on or under the ground. Unlike lizards, they have smooth skin and lack claws and ear openings. Seldom seen, they live in dark, moist habitats and are typically nocturnal and secretive. They are most active in the spring and fall, especially near the pools where they breed. Fertilization is internal, but is not accomplished by copulation. In most species, the male releases a small packet of sperm during mating. The female brushes against the packet and draws it into her body. The packet is kept in her body until she ovulates, which may be months later. Most species lay their eggs in water. Both adults and larvae are carnivorous and feed on invertebrates, worms and insects. Some salamanders have the ability to regenerate tails or limbs lost to predators.

NORTHWESTERN SALAMANDER

Ambystoma gracile
10 cm (4")

Found in moist forests and grasslands. It is identified by its grey-brown colour, large swellings behind the eyes and ridged tail. A mole salamander, it spends much of its time underground in burrows. Its diet consists of worms, insects and small animals.

LONG-TOED SALAMANDER

Ambystoma macrodactylum
18 cm (7")

Found in dry and moist habitats near water at elevations ranging from sea level to 2700 m (9000 ft.). It is identified by its dark colour and long, yellow, dorsal stripe, which may be broken into a series of spots. Spawns early in spring.

ROUGH-SKINNED NEWT

Taricha granulosa
to 10 cm (4")

This newt belongs to a family of highly terrestrial salamanders. Found in forests and grasslands near water, it is identified by its body shape, rough skin and flattened head. Its skin is dark above and yellowish below. Males are smooth-skinned during breeding season. This is the most familiar salamander in BC, as it is often active during the day.

TOADS

Both toads and frogs are squat, tail-less amphibians which are common near ponds and lakes. All have large heads and eyes, long hind legs and long, sticky tongues which they use to catch insects. Most have well-developed ears and strong voices. Only males are vocal.

Toads can be distinguished from frogs by their dry, warty skin and prominent glands behind their eyes (parotoids). Some also have swellings between their eyes (bosses). When handled roughly by would-be predators, the warts and glands secrete a poisonous substance which makes the toads extremely unpalatable. Contrary to popular belief, handling toads does not cause warts.

WESTERN TOAD

Bufo boreas
to 12 cm (4.7")

Found in valleys and meadows or forests near water. Grey-green in colour, it is distinguished by its light, dorsal stripe. Warts contrast body colour and are often tinged in rust. Active during twilight, it often lives in rodent burrows. Its trembling voice is like the peeping of chicks.

FROGS

Unlike toads, frogs have smooth skin, slim waists, prominent dorsal ridges and lack parotoid glands. Like toads, males initiate mating by calling for females. When a male finds a mate, he clasps her in water and fertilizes the eggs as they are laid. The eggs initially hatch into fishlike tadpoles which breathe through gills and feed on vegetation. They later transform into young adults and develop limbs and lungs. They feed primarily on insects and crustaceans.

WOOD FROG

Rana sylvatica
to 6 cm (2.4")

Common in damp woods and wet grasslands, it often ranges far from water after breeding in early spring. Varying in colour from brown to pink, it can be recognized by its dark eye patches, light belly and light jaw stripe. Its call is a series of short, duck-like quacks. Active primarily at night, it hibernates under forest litter during winter.

PACIFIC TREEFROG

Hyla regilla
4 cm (1.5")

Found in sheltered areas near water, from sea level to elevations over 3,000 m (10,000 ft.). A variably-coloured frog — ranging from dark green to tan — it is distinguished by its black eye stripe and large toe pads. The most commonly heard frog in BC, its call is a loud "kreck-ek," the last syllable with rising inflection.

SPOTTED FROG

Rana pretiosa
8 cm (3")

Found near ponds, lakes and marshy areas at elevations to 3,000 m (10,000 ft). A relatively large, brownish frog, it is distinguished by its spotted back and light jaw stripe extending to the shoulder. Its throat is often mottled. Active during the day, it prefers cold waters which do not support extensive plant growth. Its call is a series of short croaks.

RED-LEGGED FROG

Rana aurora
10 cm (4")

Found in damp, densely vegetated areas and woodlands. An olive-brown frog, it is distinguished by its light jaw stripe and reddish groin and legs. Primarily diurnal. Its call is a stuttering series of guttural growls lasting two to three seconds.

FISHES

What is a fish?

Fish are cold-blooded vertebrates that live in the water, have streamlined bodies covered in scales, possess fins and breathe by means of gills.

Fish are characterized by their size, shape, feeding habits and habitat preference. Given their cold-blooded nature, water temperature greatly controls their activity and rate of body functions. All have the senses of taste, sight, touch, smell and hearing, though they lack external ears. They have small brains and a two-chambered heart. The pumping action of the heart is enhanced by muscular contractions which occur as the fish swims.

Fish swim by flexing their bodies from side to side. The dorsal and anal fins act as keels and the paired fins help steer the fish and can also act as brakes. Many also possess an internal air bladder which acts as a depth regulator; by secreting gases into the bladder or absorbing gases from it, they vary the depth at which they swim.

Most fish reproduce by laying eggs freely in the water. As the female lays the eggs, the male fertilizes them by discharging milt over them. Eggs of different species may float, sink, become attached to vegetation or be buried. Survival rates are largely influenced by environmental conditions.

How to identify fishes

First, note the size, shape and colour of the fish. Are there any distinguishing field marks like the double dorsal fins of the perches, or the down-turned lips of the suckers? Is the body thin or torpedo-shaped? Note the orientation and placement of fins on the body. Consult the text to confirm identification.

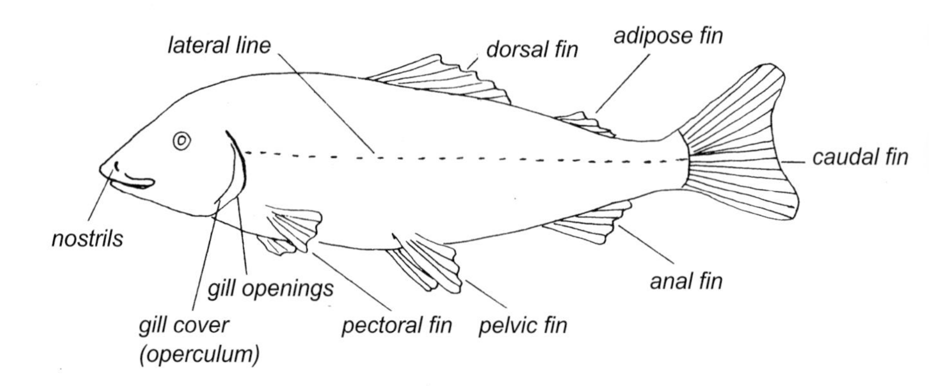

LAMPREYS

Lampreys are representatives of the most primitive order of fish. All lack jaws and feed on the blood and tissue of other fish.

PACIFIC LAMPREY

Lampetra tridentata
to 36 cm (14")

Lampreys hatch in fresh water and spend their adult life in marine habitats. Identified by their slender, eel-like bodies, round gill openings and sucker-like mouths. They feed by rasping a hole in the side of hosts with their horny teeth.

STURGEONS

Members of this prehistoric group are among the largest freshwater fishes in North America, reaching sizes up to 6 m (20 ft.) and 1450 kg (3200 lbs.). Some live for up to 150 years.

WHITE STURGEON

Acipenser transmontanus
to 3 m (10 ft.)

Found in deep pools in fresh and salt water. Size and shape are key field marks. These large, bottom-feeders are found primarily in fresh water, though some move to the ocean. All spawn in fresh water in spring.

WHITEFISH

These fork-tailed, small-headed fish are found throughout North America, Europe and Asia. All have fleshy adipose fins, large scales and few or no teeth.

LAKE WHITEFISH

Coregonus clupeaformis
to 60 cm (24")

A wide-bodied fish common in lakes throughout BC. Identified by its silvery sides, forked tail and rounded snout. Its back is often humped and the lower jaw does not extend beyond the margin of the upper jaw. Dorsal colour ranges from olive green to blue. The most important commercial fish in the province, it feeds on insects, snails and plankton.

MOUNTAIN WHITEFISH

Prosopium williamsoni
to 45 cm (18")

Abundant in streams and shallow lakes. It is distinguished by its grey-brown head and back and silvery sides. Sometimes confused with the Arctic Grayling, it has a much smaller dorsal fin. Largely a bottom feeder, it rises for surface insects on occasion.

SALMON, TROUT AND ALLIES

This diverse group includes many of the most popular sport fish in BC. Most have robust bodies, square caudal fins, an adipose fin and strong teeth. The majority are found in freshwater, though all salmon spawn in fresh water and live in salt water. The major salmon spawning runs are typically in the spring and/or fall.

COHO SALMON

Oncorhynchus kisutch
to 1 m (39")

Found near inshore waters from mid-depths to the surface. A green-blue fish, it has black spots on its back and the upper half of its caudal fin. The gums at the base of its teeth are white. Females are red-brown; spawning males have bright red sides and dark bellies.

CHINOOK SALMON (KING SALMON)

Oncorhynchus tshawytscha
to 1.5 m (5 ft.)

Inhabits the mid-depths to the surface of the open ocean. Similar to the Coho Salmon, it has irregular black spots on its back and all of its caudal fin. The gums at the base of its teeth are black. Commonly enters fresh water throughout the year. Spawning males often have blotchy, red sides.

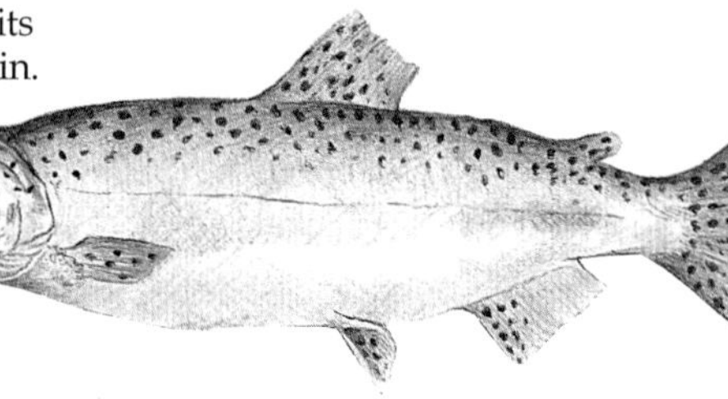

SOCKEYE SALMON (RED SALMON)

Oncorhynchus nerka
to 84 cm (33")

Found in surface waters of the open ocean. Blue-green in colour, it can be identified by its lack of large, dark spots. The spawning male has a bright red body, green head, humped back and hooked jaw. It is the most commercially valuable Pacific Salmon species. Landlocked populations are called Kokanee Salmon.

PINK SALMON

Oncorhynchus gorbuscha
to 75 cm (30")

Distinguished by large black, mostly oval, spots on its back and caudal fin. Spawning males have a deeply humped back and hooked jaw. Spawns in the fall every other year.

CHUM SALMON

Oncorhynchus keta
to 1 m (39")

This salmon lacks black spots and has a slender caudal peduncle. It is distinguished from the Sockeye by its white-edged lower fins. The spawning male has blotchy red sides. It spawns in streams close to the ocean in late fall and winter.

CUTTHROAT TROUT

Salmo clarkii
to 61 cm (24")

Found in cold streams and lakes. The distinctive red streak along the inner edge of its lower jaw is a good field mark. The throat and belly of spawners may also be reddish, while the upper half of the body is usually dark-spotted. Feeds largely on small fish.

RAINBOW TROUT (STEELHEAD)

Salmo gairdneri
to 1.2 m (4 ft.)

Abundant in streams, reservoirs and lakes. This silvery fish is named for the distinctive "rainbow" band running down its side (most prominent during spawning season — April to July). Dark spots occur along its back, upper fins and tail. The sea-run version of this species is referred to as Steelhead.

BROOK TROUT

Salvelinus fontinalis
to 56 cm (22")

This colourful fish is found in streams, ponds and shallow lakes in the mountain region. Green-purple in colour, it is distinguished by its numerous red spots (with blue haloes) and its dark-spotted dorsal fin. Note the white stripes on the leading edges of its lower fins. It feeds on a variety of invertebrates, fish and insects.

DOLLY VARDEN

Salvelinus malma
to 65 cm (26")

Found in salt and fresh water. Its greyish-green back and silvery sides are covered with red, orange and yellow spots. Note its large jaws and gently forked tail. It feeds on small fish, larvae and invertebrates. This fish is named after a Dickens' character in Barnaby Rudge who wore a spotted dress.

LAKE TROUT

Salvelinus naymaycush
to 1.2 m (48")

Found in deep, cold lakes. Its greenish-brown body is covered with numerous light spots which extend on to the dorsal and caudal fins, and its tail is deeply forked. Its diet consists of fish, crustaceans and insects, and it is known to reach weights of over 45 kg (100 lbs.).

ARCTIC GRAYLING

Thymallus arcticus
to 60 cm (24")

This fish is found in cold, clear streams and lakes. Its purplish-grey body is flecked with dark spots. It is easily distinguished by its large, mauve-spotted, dorsal fin. An aggressive fighter when hooked, it is a favourite of anglers. It feeds primarily on insects.

SMELTS

Small, slender, silvery fish found in salt and fresh water. All have a band of silver down their sides and an adipose fin.

EULACHON

Thaleichthys pacificus
to 25 cm (10")

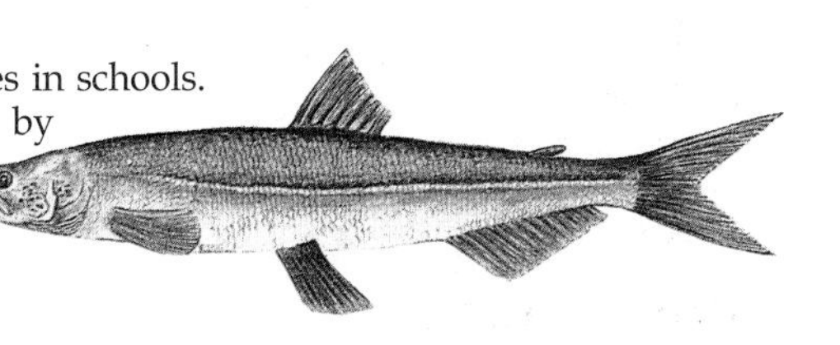

Found near shorelines in schools. They are identified by their small size, silvery side stripe and speckled back and caudal fins.

MINNOWS AND ALLIES

These fishes can be distinguished from similar species by their lack of an adipose fin and toothless jaws. The lips are typically thin and the tail is well forked.

LAKE CHUB

Couesius plumbeus
to 15 cm (6")

Very common in slow-moving streams, rivers and lakes. A rounded, lead-coloured fish, it resembles a miniature trout. Its belly is silvery or white. Males have a reddish patch at the base of their pectoral fin. Feeds largely on insects and algae.

COMMON CARP

Cyprinus carpio
to 75 cm (30")

Found in clear and turbid streams, ponds and sloughs, the Common Carp prefers warm water. A large-scaled, olive fish, it is identified by its long, single-spine dorsal fin, mouth barbels and forked caudal fin.

REDSIDE SHINER

Richardsonius balteatus
to 18 cm (7")

Found in slow-flowing streams and pools. A small, silvery fish, the Shiner is identified by its dark back and dark lateral band. During spawning in summer, both the males and females develop a red side stripe.

SUCKERS

Suckers have distinctive, fleshy lips that they use to "vacuum" the bottom of lakes and streams in search of invertebrates.

LONGNOSE SUCKER

Catostomus catostomus
to 51 cm (20")

Very common in clear, deep water in rivers and lakes throughout BC. A grey to olive-coloured fish, it is distinguished by its long snout, which extends beyond its downward pointing lips. Note the white belly and long anal fin.

WHITE SUCKER

Catostomus commersoni
to 56 cm (22")

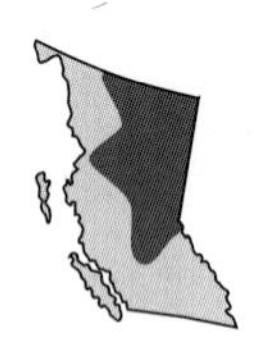

Common in warm, shallow rivers and lakes. Similar to the Longnose Sucker, it is identified by its blunt snout and dark colouration. Despite its name, it is a brown to olive-coloured fish. Feeds primarily on aquatic invertebrates and insects.

COD AND ALLIES

All have long tapering bodies and long dorsal and anal fins. Barbels are often present.

BURBOT (LING COD)

Lota lota
to 75 cm (30")

Found in the cool waters of lakes and streams throughout BC. An elongate, bottom-feeding fish, it is normally a mottled green-grey. The best field marks are its double dorsal fin and single chin whisker (barbel). It feeds on small fish, crustaceans and insects.

STICKLEBACKS

These small fishes are named for the defined row of spines along their back. Noted for their mating behaviour, the males are responsible for building intricate, suspended nests and guarding the eggs and young.

THREESPINE STICKLEBACK

Gasterosteus aculeatus
to 10 cm (4")

Found in shallow, vegetated streams and pools. This fish is identified by its slender, green/brown body and the row of three short spines ahead of the dorsal fin. The body is dark above, pale below and mottled on the sides. It feeds on crustaceans, insects and algae. Its similar cousin, the Ninespine Stickleback, has 7-11 dorsal spines.

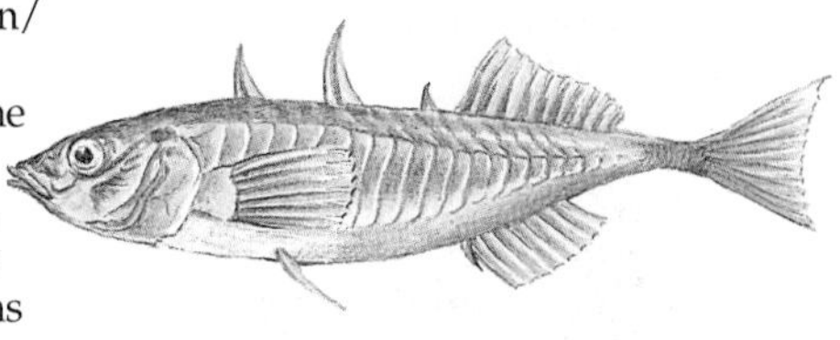

SUNFISH FAMILY

Members of this family are distinguished by double dorsal fins joined to appear as one.

PUMPKINSEED (COMMON SUNFISH)

Lepomis gibbosus
to 20 cm (8")

Found in cool, quiet, shallow waters rich in vegetation. An introduced species, it is identified by its deep body, double dorsal fins and green-orange colour. It is an aggressive fish and takes a variety of baits.

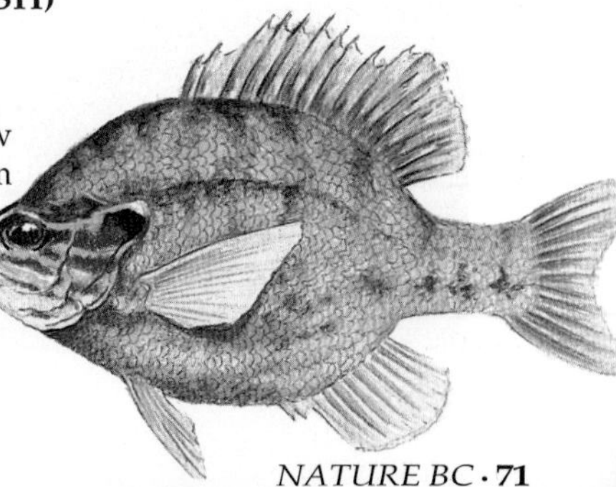

BC SHORE LIFE

What is shore life?

This section includes a mixed bag of animal and plant groups that can be found along the west coast of the province. Most species can be readily observed in tidal pools or shallow waters. All of the animals in this section are classed as invertebrates or "animals without backbones."

The best time to observe the greatest variety of species is during low tide. Tide times are often published in newspapers, and tide tables are available at most sporting goods stores. We generally have two tides a day, and tidal differences may be as much as 4.5 m (15 ft.). The lowest tides of the year occur in midwinter and midsummer.

The groups covered in this section include marine plants, sea stars and allies, crustaceans and mollusks.

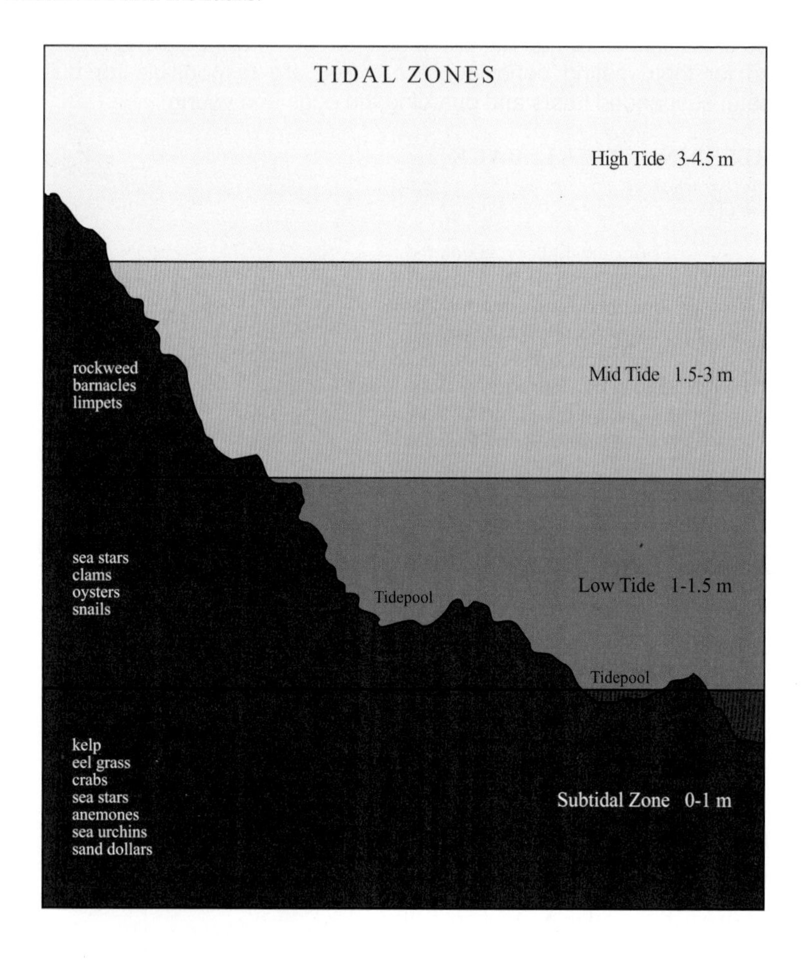

MARINE PLANTS

This general group includes a few of the most common coastal marine plants.

BULL KELP

Nereocystis luetkeana
to 20 m (65 ft.)

Found in dense beds along shorelines to depths of 30 m. The long, tubular stem is anchored to the bottom and supported by a round float. Long, bladed, brownish "leaves" (to 10 m) radiate away from the float along the water's surface. Otters are frequent inhabitants of kelp beds.

ROCKWEED

Fucus distichus
to 50 cm (20")

Very common in clumps on rocky shorelines in the intertidal zone. A widely distributed seaweed, it is a ragged, yellow-green plant with swollen air bladders along a ribbed stem. Branches are often swollen near the tip.

EELGRASS

Zostera marina
to 1.5 m (5 ft.)

Very common on muddy and sandy soils in protected waters, its leaves are flat and grass-like. Eelgrass provides a source of food and cover to many species of animals and insects and represents an important aquatic habitat.

COELENTERATES

This phylum contains a variety of free-swimming and colonial creatures including jellyfish, hydroids, anemones and corals.

BROODING ANEMONE

Epiactis prolifera
to 8 cm (3")

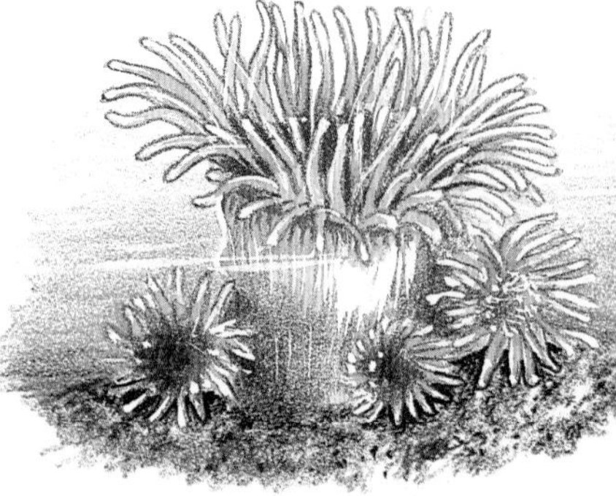

Found in low-tide zones attached to eelgrass and rocks. Identified by its flower-like profile, its terminal mouth is surrounded by up to 90 stinging tentacles which are withdrawn if disturbed. Colour ranges from red-pink to green.

SAIL JELLYFISH

Velella velella
to 10 cm (4")

Found floating on the surface of the water or washed ashore. It is identified by its bluish, translucent, bell-shaped body. Note the numerous blue tentacles around the rim of its gelatinous body. Like all jellyfish, it swims by expelling water from its mouth.

SEA STARS AND ALLIES

This group of marine, mostly bottom-dwelling animals are characterized by their spiny bodies and radial symmetry, i.e., body parts repeat around a central hub, as in a wheel. The "arms" are usually arranged in five parts, or in multiples of five. They may be short or long, cylindrical or flattened. Members of this group include sea stars, sea urchins and sand dollars.

PURPLE SEA STAR

Pisaster ochraceus
to 35 cm (14")

Common in tide pools and attached to rocks at low tide. These animals are identified by their short rays and patterned surface. They may be purple, red, yellow or brown in colour. Like salamanders, sea stars have the ability to regenerate lost body parts.

GIANT SPINED SEA STAR

Pisaster giganteus
to 60 cm (2 ft.)

Found in the low intertidal zone. Similar to the Purple Sea Star, it has much longer rays. Its deep blue colour is beautifully offset by light, delicate spines. These animals feed on shellfish and barnacles.

GREEN SEA URCHIN

Strongylocentrotus droebachiensis
to 10 cm (4")

Commonly found in shallow water attached to rocks, sea urchins are known at a glance by their rounded bodies and long spines. This species is identified by its colour. Unlike starfish, sea urchins have a hard shell and feed primarily on algae. Swimmers find them with their feet.

SAND DOLLAR

Dendraster excentricus
to 10 cm (4")

Found at low tides on sandy beaches, often partially buried. Its brown body is a hard, flat disk with short spines. Note the flowerlike impression on its shell. The shells of dead sand dollars are often found washed up on beaches.

CRUSTACEANS

Like insects, crustaceans have a hard external skeleton, antennae and paired limbs. The limbs differ greatly in form and function, and are modified for specific purposes in different species. Most live in water, though a few — e.g., sowbugs — are terrestrial. The group includes crabs, lobsters, shrimps, fairy shrimps, barnacles, water fleas and sowbugs.

PURPLE SHORE CRAB

Hemigrapsus nudas
to 4 cm (1.5")

This tiny crab is often found scuttling about on intertidal rocks. Distinguished by its deep purple body and red-spotted claws; red-brown, green and yellow variants also exist.

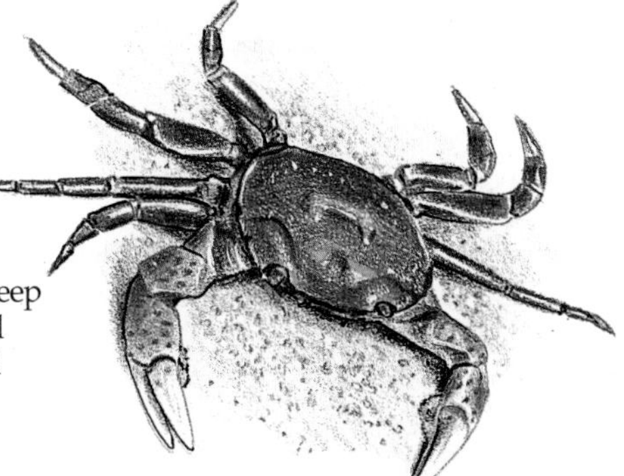

DUNGENESS CRAB

Cancer magister
to 30 cm (12")

This is the crab we commonly find in markets. Youngsters are found in sandy pools near the low-tide line; older individuals gradually migrate into deeper waters. Their colour is brown-red above and yellowish below. Though locally abundant, there is some concern that populations may be being overfished.

ACORN BARNACLE

Balanus glandula
to 2.5 cm (1")

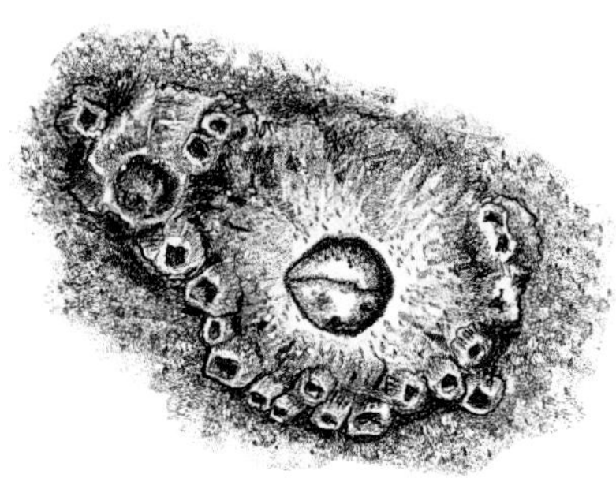

This very common barnacle is found attached to rocks and piers at the high-tide line. It is identified by the whitish-grey, heavily ribbed shell. Barnacles hatch as free-swimming larvae which eventually attach themselves to solid objects and mature into shelled adults. They feed by opening plates at the top of their shells and extending feathery "feet" to trap small organisms.

MOLLUSKS

This large group of soft-bodied, and usually hard-shelled, invertebrates occupy many habitats in water and on land. Its members include chitons, clams, oysters, snails, slugs, squids and octopuses. Mollusks grow by secreting shell material from glands near the edge of the mantle. The shape of the shell is largely determined by inheritance. The mouth of most mollusks, excluding bivalves, has a ribbon-like toothed structure called a radula which helps the animals break down food or capture prey. This group includes chitons, snails and allies, tusk shells, bivalves, and squids and allies.

WHITECAP LIMPET

Acmaea mitra
to 2.5 cm (1")

Found on rocks below the low-tide line, it is often washed ashore. Its thick, conical white shell is often covered by knobby, pink, algal growths. Unlike many other shelled creatures, its shell lacks spirals.

NATIVE LITTLENECK CLAM

Protothaca staminea
to 8 cm (3")

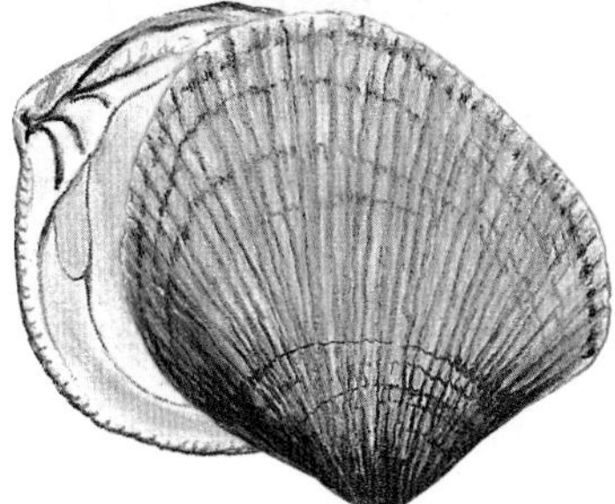

Found in sandy and gravelly soils in the mid-tide region. Their rounded, white shells are ribbed with growth lines. They feed by extracting minute particles from the water passing over their gills.

PACIFIC OYSTER

Crassostrea gigas
to 30 cm (12")

Common in the intertidal zone, it is distinguished at a glance by its heavy, irregular shell. Like other bivalves (including clams, mussels and scallops), its body is composed of two hinged shells held together by powerful muscles. Most live in sand or mud.

BLUE MUSSEL

Mytilus edulis
to 5 cm (2")

Very common in protected waters along rocky shorelines. Its blue-black shell is a smooth, wedge-shaped oval. Like barnacles, they often attach themselves to pilings and other marine objects.

PINK SCALLOP

Chlamys hastata
to 10 cm (4")

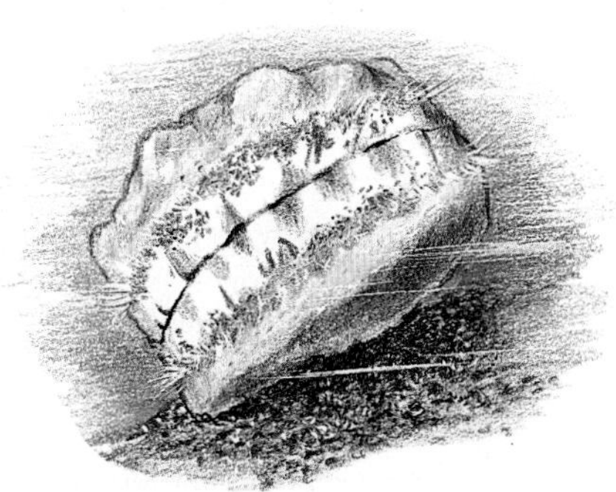

Found in intertidal waters attached to rocks. Its beautiful, fan-shaped, white shell is often covered with purplish sponge. Unlike other bivalves, scallops possess a set of eyes that line the edge of the mantle.

OTHER INVERTEBRATES

This group includes a few of the most familiar terrestrial, soft-bodied invertebrates found in BC. Snails are mollusks and related to oysters and clams. Most have coiled, cone-shaped shells, though some, like slugs, lack a shell. Water is very important to slugs since they lack a protective shell. Under dry conditions, they will curl up in the ground or under a log and secrete a protective mucous covering.

EARTHWORM

Lumbricus terrestris
to 25 cm (10")

Found in moist soils throughout the province. Distinguished by its cylindrical segmented body. Like snakes, earthworms move by contracting and elongating muscles in a wave-like fashion. Some segments have tiny bristles which provide traction. Their diet includes organic matter strained from mud. Earthworms are hermaphroditic and possess both male and female sex organs.

STRIPED SNAIL

Monadenia fidelis
to 4 cm (1.5")

Found under logs and on plants and buildings. The striking shell is typically brown with one or more dark and light bands. Its body is black and red and has a garlic odour. It feeds on fungi, dung and decaying fruits and plants.

COMMON SNAIL

Haplotrema sportella
to 2 cm (1")

Found in humid woods and gardens. It is identified by its green-yellow shell and light body. The shell has a distinctive flattened spire. All snails have lungs and breathe through a hole on the right side of their bodies.

INTRODUCED EUROPEAN SLUG

Arion ater
to 15 cm (6")

This garden slug is very common in BC. Identified by its black back covered with coarse bumps, white variants also exist. When disturbed, it has the unusual habit of contracting into a ball and rocking back and forth.

BANANA SLUG

Ariolimax columbianus
to 25 cm (10")

The banana slug is the largest slug found in western North America. It is usually some shade of greenish-yellow and has dark blotches on its body. Slugs eat primarily plants and decaying matter and are very important "recyclers" of energy and nutrients.

BC PLANTS

Based on structural and reproductive characteristics, the plants in this guide can be separated into broad classes of seed plants:

1. Gymnosperms - plants with naked seeds; and
2. Angiosperms - plants with enclosed seeds.

Gymnosperms— The Naked Seed Plants

This group of mostly evergreen trees and shrubs includes some of the largest and oldest known plants. They began to appear about 350 million years ago in the Devonian period, and were the dominant plant species on earth for some 200 million years. The most successful surviving group of gymnosperms are the conifers, which include such species as pines, spruces, firs, larches and junipers.

The term "gymnosperm" means naked seed, and all members of this group produce fruit (usually woody cones) with naked seeds. Commonly called "coniferous" or "softwood" trees, most species are evergreen and have small needle-like or scale-like leaves which are adapted to withstand extreme variances in temperature and the abrasions of storms. Some species are deciduous, but most retain their leaves for two or more years before shedding them.

Reproduction

To better understand the naked seed method of reproduction, let us look at the life cycle of a conifer.

Unlike angiosperms, conifers lack flowers or fruits. Most bear seeds on the inner edge of scale-like leaves which are usually arranged spirally to form a woody cone. Each species produces two types of spores, each in a different type of cone (male or female). The spores produced in the male cones develop into winged pollen grains, and these are blown by the wind to eventually fall between the scales of female cones on other trees. The smaller male cones are usually located on the bottom branches of a tree, while the larger female cones are located higher up – likely an adaptation that prevents a tree from pollinating itself. After fertilization, the female spore develops into a seed. When the seed is fully matured, it falls away from the cone and is blown about by the wind. If it reaches favourable ground in proper conditions, it germinates. In pines, it takes as much as a year between pollination and fertilization, and several years may elapse after fertilization until the seeds are shed.

Angiosperms — The Flowering Plants

Angiosperms first appeared in the fossil record about 130 million years ago. Over the next 60 million years they quickly adapted to a wide variety of environments, and by the end of the Cretaceous Period (see **Geological Time Scale** page 3) they had succeeded gymnosperms as the dominant land plants. Their reproductive success was largely owing to two key adaptations:

1. they produced flowers to aid in pollen dispersal; and
2. they produced seeds encased in "fruits", to aid in seed dispersal.

Angiosperms make up a diverse and widespread group of flowering plants ranging from trees and shrubs like the oaks, cherries, maples, hazelnuts and apples, to the more typical "flowers" like lilies, orchids, roses, daisies and violets. Together they provide us with much of our food and shelter, and add colour and aroma to a vast array of settings. The trees and shrubs within this group are commonly referred to as "deciduous," "broadleaf," or "hardwoods," and all shed their leaves annually.

Reproduction

The single most important adaptation that allowed angiosperms to succeed gymnosperms as the dominant land plants was the development of "flowers."

Flowers are simply modified stems which have evolved into alluring structures for attracting pollinating agents such as insects and birds. A typical flower consists of four sets of leaves attached to the expanded end of the stem, calledthe receptacle. The outermost leaves, usually green and leaf-like, are called sepals. The often showy, colourful leaves above the sepals which attract pollinating agents are called petals. In flowers which lack petals, the sepals may be colourful and petal-like.

Inside the petals are the male parts of the flower, the stamens. Stamens are composed of thin filaments supporting anthers containing pollen. In the centre of the flower is the female reproductive structure, the pistil. The pistil is composed of a swollen basal part called the ovary, a narrow neck called the style and the opening in the style called the stigma. Fertilization occurs when pollen — carried by the wind, insects, or animals — reaches the unfertilized eggs (ovules) in the ovary. After fertilization, the ovules mature into seeds.

It is important to note that angiosperms vary greatly between species with regard to the shape, position, and number of different parts. Flowers having both stamens and pistils are referred to as perfect flowers. Those which lack organs of one sex are referred to as imperfect flowers.

Once fertilization has occurred, the ovary begins to develop into a fruit. At this point the sepals, petals, stamens and style usually fall off the flower head. The fruit and ovules mature together, with the fruit ripening at the point the seeds are capable of germinating. Each seed within itself contains an embryo and a food supply to nourish it upon germination. Upon ripening, the fruit may fall to the ground with the

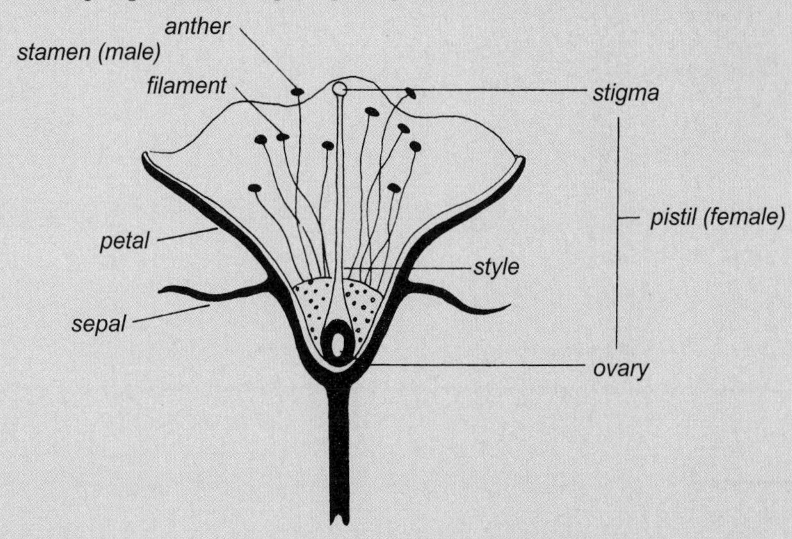

seeds still inside it, as in peaches, cherries, and squash, or it may burst open and scatter its seeds in the wind, like poplar trees, pussy willows and dandelions.

Fruit comes in many forms, from fleshy berries, grapes, apples and pears, to pea and bean pods, nuts, burrs, capsules, tomatoes and kernels. Regardless of the shape it takes, fruit enhances the reproductive success of angiosperms in two important ways. First, it helps to protect the seeds from the elements until they have fully matured, enabling them to survive unfavourable conditions (like winter). Secondly, fruit aids in seed dispersal. Some fruits are eaten by animals that eventually release the seeds in their faeces, an ideal growing medium. Others may be spiny or burred so they catch on the coats of animals, or may have special features which enable them to be carried away from their parent plant by the wind or water.

Angiosperms have evolved into two groups — monocots and dicots — which differ from each other in stem and leaf anatomy, embryonic leaf structure, and flower form. Simply put, the monocots make up most other cereal plants like wheat, rice, barley, and corn, in addition to grasses, lilies and irises. Dicots generally comprise most fruit and vegetables like tomatoes, beans, potatoes and carrots, as well as willows, maples, elms, buttercups and dandelions. Most of the plants discussed in this guide are dicots. Each group can be compared and contrasted according to the following features:

Monocots — one embryonic leaf at germination, parallel veined leaves, flower parts (e.g., petals, sepals and stamens) occur in threes or multiples of three, stem is composed of irregularly distributed fibres.

Dicots — two embryonic leaves at germination, net-veined leaves, flower parts occur in fours, fives or multiples of these, stem is composed of uniformly distributed fibres, forming rings in many cases.

BC TREES

What is a tree?

Trees can be broadly defined as perennial woody plants at least 5 m (16 ft.) tall, which have a single stem and a well-developed crown of branches, twigs and leaves. Most are long-lived plants and range in age from 40-50 years for deciduous trees, to several hundred years for many of the conifers.

The size and shape of a tree is largely determined by its genetic makeup, but its growth is also affected by environmental factors such as moisture, light and competition from other species. Trees growing in crowded stands will often only support compact crowns of leaves and branches, owing to competition for light. Some species grow gnarled and twisted at higher elevations, owing to a short growing season and constant exposure to high winds.

How to identify trees

First, note the size and shape. Many species have characteristic shapes and can be distinguished from a distance by their silhouettes. Next, note the colour and texture of the bark and the arrangement of the twigs. Examine the size, colour and shape of the leaves and how they are arranged on the twigs. Are they opposite or alternate? Simple or compound? Hairy or smooth? Are flowers or fruits visible on the upper branches? Once you've collected as much visual information as you can, consult the illustrations and text to confirm identification. (See page 81 for flower characteristics.)

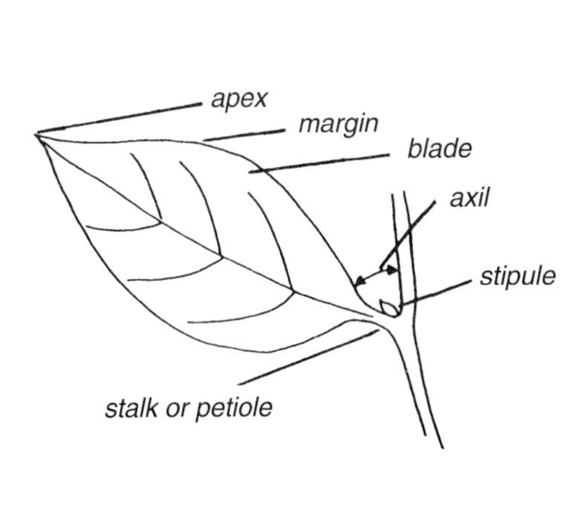

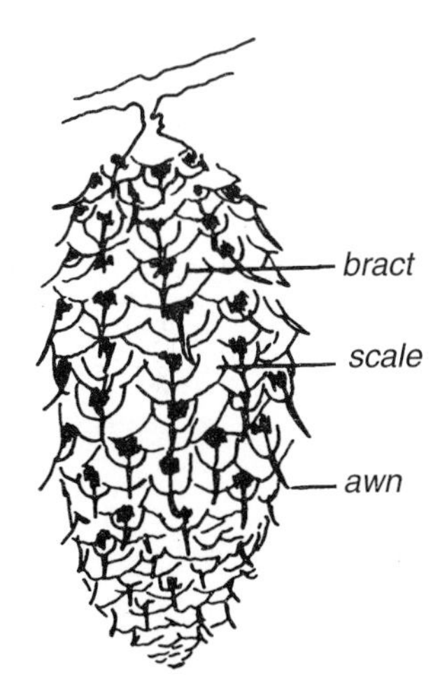

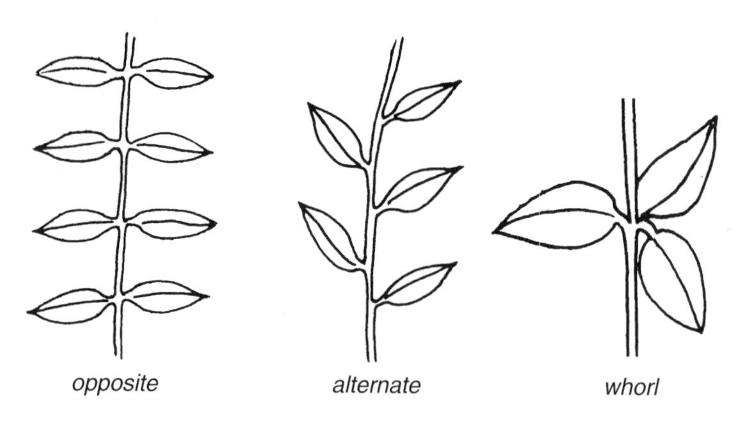

LEAF ARRANGEMENT

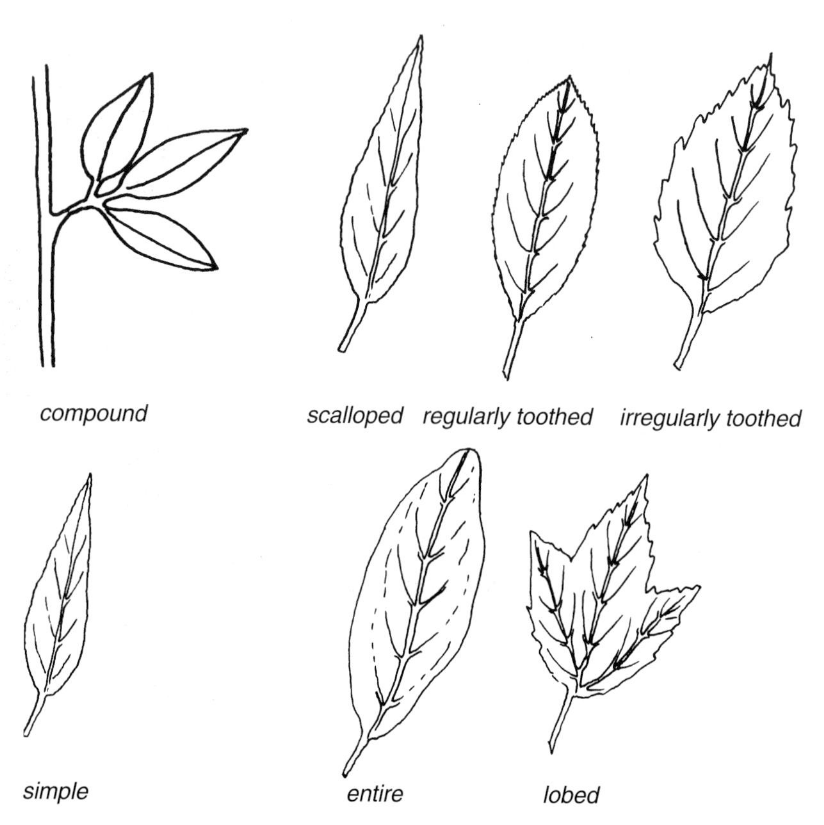

LEAF TYPES

LEAF MARGIN CHARACTERISTICS

PINES

Trees and shrubs in this group are very common throughout BC. Most are resin-bearing and have long, needle-like leaves which are grouped together in bundles. Male and female cones usually occur on the same tree. Important commercially, they are responsible for the majority of the lumber, pulp and paper produced in the province. Many are valuable sources of food and cover for wildlife.

WHITEBARK PINE

Pinus albicaulis
3-10 m (10-33 ft.)

A small alpine tree found on rocky soil at high altitudes (above 1100 m) in the mountains. The short, stout trunk supports an irregular crown of spreading branches. The bark is greyish and deeply furrowed in mature trees. Stiff needles occur in clusters of five and are densely packed at the end of twigs. The scales of its oval, thick cones (3-5 cm) are armed with a hard point at their tip. It grows prostrate in exposed locations.

WESTERN WHITE PINE

Pinus monticola
15-50 m (50-160 ft.)

Found in mountain regions at middle and upper elevations, its conical crown of horizontally growing branches is often open and ragged. Its long, blue-green needles (5-13 cm) are arranged in clusters of five. The stalked, elongated cones (to 22 cm) may be gently curved. The Western White Pine is distinguished from other conifers by its long needles and cones.

LODGEPOLE PINE

Pinus contorta
20-40 m (65-130 ft.)

Found in a variety of habitats, it is one of BC's most common trees. The crown is ragged, and its slender trunk is often barren when shaded. Trees growing on the margins of boggy areas are shorter and more shrub-like in appearance. Their stiff needles (2-5 cm) are twisted in bundles of two, and the cone scales have a single prickle near their outer edge. It is named for its straight, narrow trunk, which the Indians used for teepee poles.

LARCHES

Unlike most conifers, larches are deciduous and shed their leaves in the fall. Their needles grow from woody pegs along twigs in large clusters of 10-40. Their cones grow away from branches, often upright and are usually retained for more than one year. Larches can easily be distinguished from other conifers in autumn by their yellow-gold needles.

ALPINE LARCH

Larix occidentalis
to 50 m (160 ft.)

Found in southeastern BC on moist and dry soils, its yellow-green needles (3 cm) occur in bunches of 12-24. Its red-brown bark grows in thick, elongate plates. The small, upright cones (2-4 cm) have long, protruding bracts.

SPRUCES

These relatively large evergreens are commonly found on moist soils. Clusters of four-sided needles grow from woody pegs along the branches. Cones are pendant and often grow in clusters. You can quickly check for spruce in the field by rolling the needles between your fingers; four-sided needles roll much easier than two-sided needles.

WHITE SPRUCE

Picea glauca
to 30 m (100 ft.)

Common throughout much of the province, it is often confused with the Engelmann Spruce, which grows at higher elevations. The tall, straight trunk supports a uniform crown of spreading branches. Its grey-brown bark is often blistered by resin. The blue-green needles (to 3 cm) are sharply pointed and tend to twist upward. Its hard, cylindrical cones have stiff scales with smooth, rounded outer edges.

ENGELMANN SPRUCE

Picea engelmann
to 40 m (130 ft.)

Widespread throughout the foothills and mountains at elevations above 1100 m, it is common in southern BC. In dense stands, the long, barren trunk supports a compact conical crown. The branchlets are covered with soft hairs, and the silvery-green needles have blunt, flattened tips and exude a pungent odour when crushed. It can be distinguished by its hairy branchlets and ragged, flexible cones, and often grows dwarfed at high, windswept elevations.

SITKA SPRUCE

Picea sitchensis
to 90 m (300 ft.)

Found at low elevations along the coast, BC's Carmanah Valley is home to the largest members of this group. Typical species are 30-45 m tall. Its needles are flat, very prickly and bristle in all directions. The ragged cone has loose, thin, irregular scales.

HEMLOCKS

Hemlocks are distinguished quickly by their delicate foliage and drooping tips. Needles are two-sided and grow singly from woody pegs along the branches.

WESTERN HEMLOCK

Tsuga heterophylla
to 50 m (160 ft.)

Identified at a distance as a large tree (to 55 m) with a drooping tip. It grows well in shaded areas. The needles (1.5 cm) are flat and bear two light lines on the underside. Short cones (to 3 cm) are attached directly to the twigs. The similar Mountain Hemlock (*Tsuga mertensia*) found along the coast, is distinguished by its smaller size (to 30 m) and longer cones (to 6 cm).

FIRS

Firs are medium-sized evergreens with dense, symmetrical crowns. The bark of young trees is smooth and often blistered by resin; mature bark is furrowed and scaly. Flattened, stalkless needles grow singly and bear a longitudinal scar from base to tip. Cones grow upright from the branches and disintegrate when the seeds are ripe. After the cone scales are shed, a central, candle-like stalk remains on the branch.

ALPINE FIR

Abies lasiocarpa
to 25 m (80 ft.)

Common in alpine forests at elevations above 1100 m. The uniform, conical crown is composed of short, thick branches. The dark green needles have silvery lines on both surfaces and are flattened on the lower branches. Its cylindrical cones grow erect and have fan-shaped scales. Exposed trees are often low and gnarled and the tree may form a dense "hedge" if its lower branches take root.

DOUGLAS-FIRS

Larger than true firs, they are also identified by their slender stemmed needles.

DOUGLAS-FIR

Pseudotsuga menziesii
30-75 m (100-250 ft.)

A common tree found throughout southern BC. Its needles (to 3 cm) bristle in all directions from the branch. It is easily identified by cones that have three-pronged "pitchfork" bracts extending far beyond the scales. Its trunk is bare when growing in shaded areas or dense stands.

CEDARS

All have scaly or awl-shaped leaves which are tightly bunched together on twigs. The heavily weighted twigs usually droop at their tips and give the plants a relaxed profile. The wood of most is very fragrant.

WESTERN RED CEDAR

Thuja plicata
to 60 m (200 ft.)

Common on moist soil in the coastal and interior regions. Leaves grow in tight pairs along the branches and are smooth to the touch. Small cones (2 cm) stand erect on its branches and are present throughout the winter. The reddish bark is shredded and fibrous. A very important commercial species, it is our provincial tree.

YELLOW CEDAR

Chamaecyparis nootkatensis
to 30 m (100 ft.)

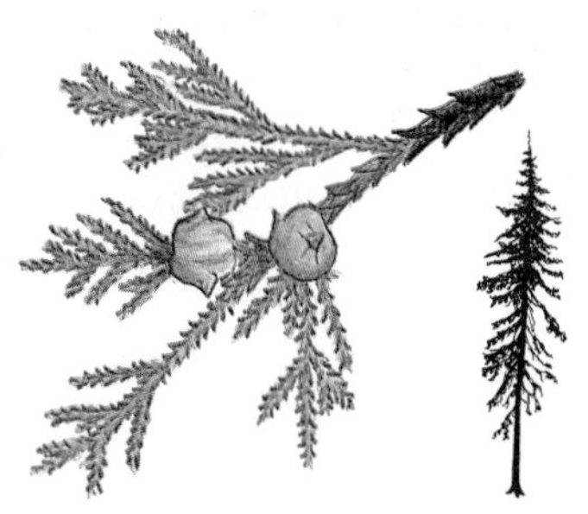

Common along the coast from Oregon to Alaska, its leaves are similar to red cedar but are prickly to the touch, especially when stroked against the grain. Its cones are round with wedge-shaped scales. The shaggy, greyish bark occurs in thin, vertical scales with loose ends.

YEWS

Yews are a primitive race of small, needle-leaved evergreen trees that lack woody cones.

WESTERN YEW

Taxus brevifolia
5-15 m (15-50 ft.)

Found at low elevations on moist soil in the coastal and interior regions. Sharp, flat needles (to 3 cm) grow singly from the twigs and have two silvery stripes below. Its reddish-purple bark is scaly and breaks off in irregular strips. Distinctive greenish seeds protrude from its scarlet berries in autumn.

ANGIOSPERMS

WILLOWS

This large family of deciduous trees and shrubs is widely distributed throughout the province. Found largely on moist soils, they are abundant along streams, rivers and lakes. Most have narrow, finely-toothed leaves which grow alternately along twigs. Flowers often appear in spring before the leaves along semi-erect catkins. After pollination, flowers are succeeded by small pods. When ripe, these pods burst open and shed numerous "cottony" seeds in the wind.

PACIFIC WILLOW

Salix lasiandra
to 15 m (50 ft.)

Found at lower elevations near water sources, it is distinguished at a distance by its irregular crown of ascending branches. The finely toothed, narrow leaves (to 12 cm) are dark green above, greyish below and may be twisted to the side. The bark is blackish and furrowed into irregular plates. Its catkins shed their cottony seeds in summer.

WEEPING WILLOW

Salix babylonica
to 15 m (50 ft.)

Native to China, this introduced willow is widely planted as an ornamental throughout BC. Easily distinguished by its short trunk and wide crown of drooping ("weeping") branches. Narrow, finely-toothed leaves are evident from early spring until late autumn.

POPLARS

Found in moist habitats, these fast-growing trees are common throughout most of the province. They are distinguished from willows at a glance by their drooping catkins. Their alternate, un-lobed leaves are toothed, generally heart-shaped and usually as long as they are broad. The green-white bark of young trees becomes greyish and furrowed as it matures.

TREMBLING ASPEN

Populus tremuloides
to 30 m (100 ft.)

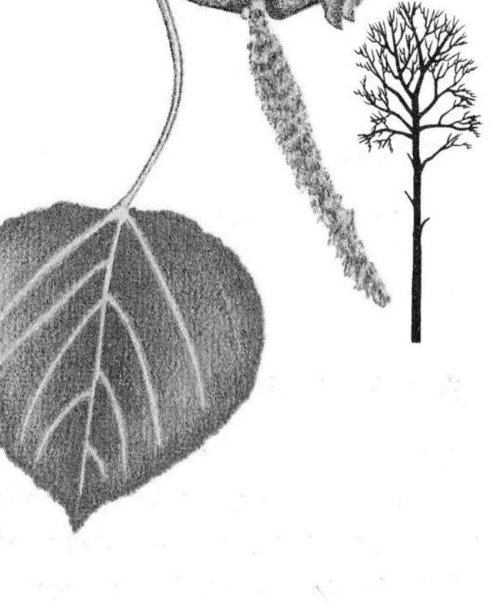

Very common east of the Cascades. Its long, slender trunk supports a compact, rounded crown of spreading branches. Its rounded leaves have greenish surfaces, silvery undersides and are finely toothed. The leaf stalks are usually longer than the leaves themselves and the leaves will rustle in the slightest breeze. The greenish-white bark becomes riddled with black, wartlike marks as it ages. Its twigs, leaves, catkins and bark are an important food source to several animal and bird species throughout the year.

BLACK COTTONWOOD

Populus trichocarpa
to 30 m (100 ft.)

Common and widespread on moist soils throughout BC. The long trunk supports a broad crown of ascending branches. Its dark green leaves are oval to heart-shaped, finely toothed and have unusually long stems. The bark on mature trees is grey and deeply furrowed, forming rough, flat-topped ridges on the trunk. Its branches are greyish-brown. The nearly identical Balsam Poplar *(Populus balsamifera)* is found in the northeast corner of BC. Both shed their cottony seeds in spring.

BIRCHES

Most members of this family occur as shrubs in BC. In all, the male and female flowers occur in catkins on the same plant. The alternate leaves are commonly oval-shaped with prominently toothed margins. Cylindrical cones (strobiles) disintegrate in the fall when ripe. The fruit is either a winged nutlet or a nut enclosed in a leafy case. All are fast growing and short-lived.

PAPER BIRCH

Betula papyrifera
to 25 m (80 ft.)

Common on moist soil in forested regions of BC. The straight trunk supports a rounded to conical crown of ascending branches. Its dull green leaves are irregularly toothed (except near their base), and have five to nine straight side veins. The smooth bark is whitish to red-brown and peels off easily in thin sheets. It thrives in burned-out and cut-over areas where it quickly reproduces by suckering. Indians once used birch bark to construct lightweight canoes.

HAWTHORNS

Hawthorns are of thorny shrubs and trees.

BLACK HAWTHORN

Crataegus douglasii
to 20 m (65 ft.)

Found in wet areas along streams and meadows. Its leaves are coarsely toothed on the upper half. The twigs zigzag and often form impenetrable thickets. Distinguished as a round bushy tree with sharp spines. Its bark is grey and scaly. Showy clusters of white flowers bloom in May, followed by small, purplish, apple-like fruits (1 cm in diameter) in summer.

ALDERS

Alders are fast-growing shrubs and trees with ragged crowns and prominently veined leaves. Members of the birch family, they are distinguished by their fruits, which harden into woody cones and root structures that are able to absorb nitrogen from the air (allowing the plant to survive on nutrient-poor soils).

SITKA ALDER

Alnus sinuata
to 9 m (30 ft.)

Found throughout BC at elevations above 900 m. Typically a sprawling shrub with crooked ascending limbs. Glossy green leaves are finely toothed (to 10 cm). The cone-like strobiles do not disintegrate upon maturing. The grey-green bark is often flecked with light-coloured, warty lenticels.

MOUNTAIN ALDER

Alnus tenuifolia
to 7 m (23 ft.)

Large shrub or small tree commonly found on moist soil bordering swamps, streams and lakes. The bark on mature branches is red-orange and smooth. Alternating dark green leaves are sharply serrated and have an orange-yellow central vein. Woody, cone-like fruits appear in fall and remain on the shrub until the following summer.

CHERRIES

Trees and shrubs which produce fragrant flower clusters followed by small fleshy berries. All have alternate leaves.

BITTER CHERRY

Prunus emarginata
to 12 m (40 ft.)

Found in dry to moist soil in the coastal region. Its leaves are oval or lance-shaped and taper to a point (to 8 cm). White flowers bloom in April and May in round, flat-topped clusters of 5-10 and are followed by small, bright red, summer berries (1 cm in diameter). The berries are edible, but the stones should never be swallowed; the stones and leaves of all *Prunus* species contain cyanide.

CHOKE CHERRY

Prunus virginiana
2-6 m (6-20 ft.)

A bushy shrub or tree found along streams, wooded margins and brushy slopes. Light green, alternate leaves are smooth-sided and sharply toothed. The trunk is often twisted, and the reddish-grey bark smells bitter when bruised. Flowers bloom in dense cylindrical clusters in April to May. Its blackish berries mature in late summer and make excellent jams and jellies.

APPLES

A single native crab-apple tree is common in BC.

PACIFIC CRAB APPLE

Malus diversifolia
to 10 m (33 ft.)

Found in moist areas along the western edge of the province. Often shrub-like, it is very bushy when growing in the open. Its thick leaves are sharply toothed, prominently veined and usually ovate, though a variety of shapes occur. White blossoms appear in April-May and are followed by oblong yellow-to-red apples (2 cm) July-Oct.

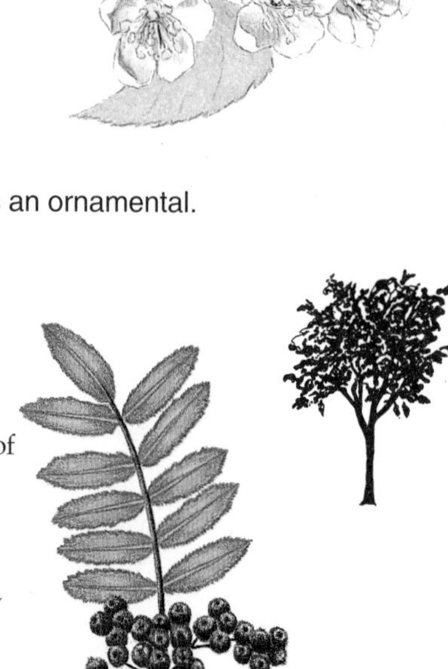

MOUNTAIN ASH

This introduced species is widely planted as an ornamental.

EUROPEAN MOUNTAIN ASH

Sorbus aucuparia
to 10 m (33 ft.)

A common shrub or tree, the trunk(s) support an open crown of spreading branches. Alternate, compound leaves have 9-15 leaflets and are bluntly toothed. White flowers bloom in dense clusters in early spring. These are succeeded by the familiar flattened clusters of red berries which persist into winter. Winter buds are covered with a coat of fine, whitish hairs. The berries are a favourite food of waxwings.

MAPLES

Maples are distinguished by their large, opposite growing leaves and long-winged seed pairs. The leaves are especially conspicuous in autumn when they turn vivid shades of orange and red before falling off. BC's maples do not produce usable syrup.

DOUGLAS MAPLE

Acer glabrum var. douglasii
to 10 m (33 ft.)

Common in moist locations along streams and sheltered slopes. Most occur as small shrubs with short trunks and irregular crowns. Opposing leaves have three to five lobes and saw-toothed edges. Twigs and leaf stems are usually bright red. Winged seed pairs are green or pinkish on the tree, turning brown in autumn. Its smooth bark is red-brown to grey.

HEATHS

A large group of trees, shrubs and flowering plants which inhabit acidic soils in temperate regions.

ARBUTUS

Arbutus menziesii
to 30 m (100 ft.)

A distinctive tree found in the Gulf Islands region of the province. Glossy-green, leathery leaves grow alternately (to 15 cm). Its most distinctive field mark is its smooth, red-orange bark, which is exposed when the outer bark peels off. Clusters of white flowers bloom in April-May and are followed by red-orange berries in July - Oct.

BC SHRUBS

What is a shrub?

Shrubs are perennial woody plants normally less than 5 m (16 ft.) tall which support a crown of branches, twigs and leaves. Unlike trees they are anchored to the ground by several stems, rather than a single trunk. Most are fast-growing and an important source of food and shelter for wildlife.

How to identify shrubs

First, note the size and shape. Many species have characteristic shapes and can be distinguished from a distance by their silhouettes. Next, note the colour and texture of the bark and the arrangement of the twigs. Examine the size, colour and shape of the leaves and how they are arranged on the twigs. Are they opposite or alternate? Simple or compound? Hairy or smooth? Are flowers or fruits visible on the upper branches? Once you've collected as much visual information as you can, consult the illustrations and text to confirm identification. (See pages 81 and 84 for leaf and flower characteristics.)

SHRUBS WITH RED-ORANGE BERRIES

KINNIKINNICK (BEARBERRY)

Arctostaphylos uva-ursi
to 60 cm (2 ft.)

A mat-forming shrub found on coarse and gravelly soils throughout BC. Its alternating, evergreen leaves are leathery and paddle-shaped. Small, pinkish, bell-shaped flowers bloom in drooping clusters in summer. Bright red berries are visible throughout autumn and are a favourite food of bears and birds.

THIMBLEBERRY

Rubus parviflorus
to 2 m (6 ft.)

Found on moist soils along the borders of woods and thickets. The large, velvety, maple-like leaves (to 25 cm) are a good field mark. Large, white, rose-like flowers (to 5 cm) bloom in June-July and are followed by lumpy, red berries.

SALMONBERRY

Rubus spectabilis
to 4 m (13 ft.)

Common as a shrub or thicket near water at low elevations. Leaflets occur in threes and are a good field mark. Its bark is satiny brown and covered with sparse thorns. Showy, papery, pinkish flowers (to 3 cm) bloom in April-May, followed by salmon to red raspberry-like fruits.

LOW-BUSH CRANBERRY

Viburnum edule
to 2 m (6 ft.)

Common in moist woodlands throughout the province. Leaves are triple-lobed, deeply veined, and hairy underneath. White flowers bloom in June and are densely clustered at the tips of branches. Bright red berries appear in summer. The similar High-bush Cranberry can be distinguished by its larger size (to 4 m), and more deeply-lobed leaves.

WILD RED RASPBERRY

Rubus idaeus
to 1.5 m (5 ft.)

Common along roadsides, streams, and forest margins at low to middle elevations. Its compound leaves have three to five oblong leaflets that are evenly toothed and hairy beneath. The main stems and branches are covered in small prickles. Whitish flowers bloom in April-June. Bright red raspberry fruits appear in late summer.

CANADIAN BUFFALO-BERRY (SOAPBERRY)

Shepherdia canadensis
to 4 m (12 ft.)

Sprawling shrub common throughout the forest regions of BC. Opposing, oval leaves have waxy green surfaces and silvery, brown-spotted undersides. Small clusters of yellowish flowers bloom along leafy stems in May-June. Bright red berries succeed the flowers in early summer. When the berries are rubbed between the hands, they form a soapy froth.

SUMAC

Rhus glabra
to 2 m (6 ft.)

A branching, "crooked" shrub found on dry soils in southern BC. Its long, toothed leaves are plume-like and each has 10-30 leaflets. The plant is easily distinguished in the fall when its leaves turn vivid red and yellow. Purplish flowers bloom around April in tight conical clusters and are succeeded in the fall by red, hairy fruits. This BC species of sumac is non-poisonous.

RED-BERRY ELDER

Sambucus racemosa
to 5 m (16 ft.)

This common shrub is found in moist and shaded areas to subalpine elevations. Opposing leaves have five to seven leaflets and are sharply pointed and toothed (to 12 cm). Yellow-white flowers bloom in rounded clusters in May and are followed by red berries in June. Two similar species of elder which are found in BC have blue or black berries.

SHRUBS WITH BLUE-BLACK BERRIES

COMMON JUNIPER

Juniperus communis
to 1.5 m (5 ft.)

This low, mat-forming plant has the widest distribution of any tree or shrub in the northern hemisphere. In BC, it is common on rocky soil along forest margins and open slopes. Spreading, needle-like leaves are green below, whitish above and occur in groups of three along the branches. Berry-like cones are dark blue with a pale bloom. Varieties of this species are commonly portrayed in landscape painting.

RED-FLOWER CURRANT

Ribes sanguineum
to 3 m (10 ft.)

Found in a variety of habitats from open, wooded areas to dry, rocky locales, this is commonly planted as an ornamental shrub. Rounded leaves have three to five lobes (to 10 cm), are marked with light dots above and are finely haired below. Small, red, showy flowers bloom in early spring; berries are blue-black with a light bloom.

BLACK TWINBERRY (BRACTED HONEYSUCKLE)

Lonicera involucrata
to 1 m (3 ft.)

An erect, low-growing shrub commonly found on moist soil in open woodlands and meadows. Its opposing oval leaves are deeply veined. Paired, yellowish, tubular flowers bloom in May-June and have distinctive short leaves (bracts) at their base. As the purplish-black paired berries appear, the bracts change from green to red.

CANADA HUCKLEBERRY

Vaccinium myrtilloides
to 40 cm (16")

Found in sandy soils and swampy areas throughout central and southern BC. Its oblong, smooth-margined leaves are sharply pointed (to 4 cm). Bell-shaped, green-white flowers bloom in clusters at the ends of branches and are succeeded by blue berries with a white bloom. The berries are very sweet and ripen in August.

TALL MAHONIA

Berberis aquifolium
to 1.5 m (5 ft.)

Found in dry forests and rocky clearings and roadsides, it grows as an erect or crawling shrub. Glossy green, leathery leaves have five to seven coarsely-toothed leaflets. Bright yellow flower clusters bloom in late spring and are succeeded by dark blue berries in summer. The bark is yellowish.

SASKATOON SERVICEBERRY

Amelanchier alnifolia
to 6 m (20 ft.)

Also called Western Serviceberry, it is common in moist valleys and open wooded areas throughout BC. A shrub or small tree, it often grows in dense thickets. Alternate, leathery leaves are coarsely toothed above the middle. Whitish, star-shaped spring flowers bloom in multiple clusters at the ends of branchlets in April. Juicy, purplish-black berries appear in early summer.

SHRUBS WITH WHITISH BERRIES

RED OSIER DOGWOOD

Cornus stolonifera
to 2 m (6 ft.)

A sprawling, thicket-forming shrub common in forests, moist meadows and along waterways and roadsides. Opposing leaves have sunken veins and reddish stalks. Greenish-white, dainty flowers bloom in dense, flattened clusters in June. Waxy, whitish berries appear in late summer. The bright red bark is an excellent field mark throughout the year.

SNOWBERRY

Symphoricarpos albus
to 2 m (6 ft.)

A low, spreading shrub commonly found in wooded areas. Its thin, opposing leaves are smooth or wavy-toothed and have hairy undersides. Pink to white, bell-shaped flowers bloom in clusters near the ends of twigs in early summer. The flowers are succeeded by waxy, white berries that persist into early winter.

SILVERBERRY

Elaeagnus commutata
to 4 m (12 ft.)

An erect shrub common on dry soil on fields and hillsides throughout BC. Stiff, curled leaves have a shiny, silvery surface. Yellowish flowers bloom in small clusters along stems in June-July. These are succeeded by silvery, tough berries containing a single seed. Also referred to as "Wolf Willow."

SHRUBS LACKING BERRIES

SCOULER WILLOW

Salix scouleriana
to 6 m (20 ft.)

A small tree or shrub found in a wide range of habitats throughout the province. The straight trunk supports a rounded crown. Its blunt-tipped leaves are dark-green above, red-woolly below and widest beyond their middle, and the branches are brown to yellow-brown and often covered with fine hairs.

BEBB'S WILLOW

Salix bebbiana
to 5 m (15 ft.)

A small tree or shrub found in mixed woods and along rivers and lakes. Its crown is typically rounded. The slender leaves (to 6 cm) are light green above, light below and often toothed above the middle. Its green-grey bark may sometimes have red highlights.

LABRADOR TEA

Ledum groenlandicum
to 1 m (3 ft.)

A shrub common at middle elevations in moist coniferous forests and peatlands. The narrow, leathery leaves are red-woolly below, and have rolled margins. The erect, reddish stems are finely haired. Clusters of small white flowers bloom at the stem tips in June-July, followed by dried, hairy fruits. The leaves have been used as a tea substitute since the times of the early settlers.

MOCK ORANGE

Philadelphus lewisii
to 2 m (6 ft.)

Found at low elevations on moist and rocky soils, often in shaded areas. The light green leaves have a few teeth on either side and three main veins. Its bark is reddish-brown. Easily distinguished by its showy orange-white blossoms in June.

COMMON WILD ROSE

Rosa nutkana
to 3 m (10 ft.)

This is likely the most common "bushy" rose of the six similar species found in BC. Branches and stems are densely covered with soft prickles. Its compound leaves have an odd number of leaflets. Reddish-pink, yellow-centred flowers (to 9 cm) bloom from May to July; fruits are capsule-like "hips" which stay on the plant throughout winter.

SHRUBBY CINQUEFOIL

Potentilla fruticosa
to 1 m (3 ft.)

This erect or spreading shrub is common in a variety of habitats from rocky fields to moist meadows. Its grey-green leaves are divided into three to seven wedge-shaped leaflets which are slightly hairy, with smooth margins. Bright yellow, buttercup-like flowers bloom from June to September. Because of their long blooming period, they are widely planted as ornamentals.

BEAKED HAZELNUT

Corylus cornuta
to 4 m (13 ft.)

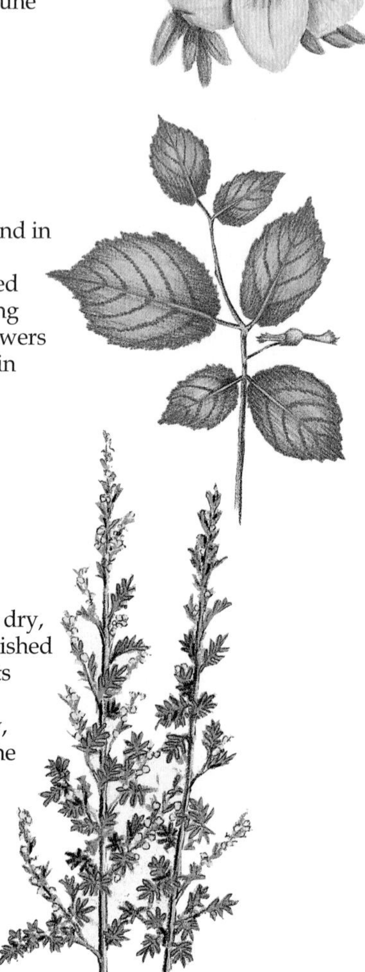

A bushy, erect shrub commonly found in open woodlands and rocky places. Alternate leaves have sharply toothed margins and are haired beneath along the veins. Inconspicuous pinkish flowers and hanging yellow catkins appear in spring before the leaves. Its nut-like fruits mature within hairy, leafy sheaths and ripen into edible filberts by autumn.

SAGEBRUSH

Artemisia tridentata
to 1.2 m (4 ft.)

This mat-forming shrub is found on dry, rocky soils and grasslands. Distinguished by its gnarled profile at a distance, its distinctive small leaves are triple-notched on the outside edge. Its tiny, yellow flowers bloom in autumn. The plant has a strong "sage" aroma.

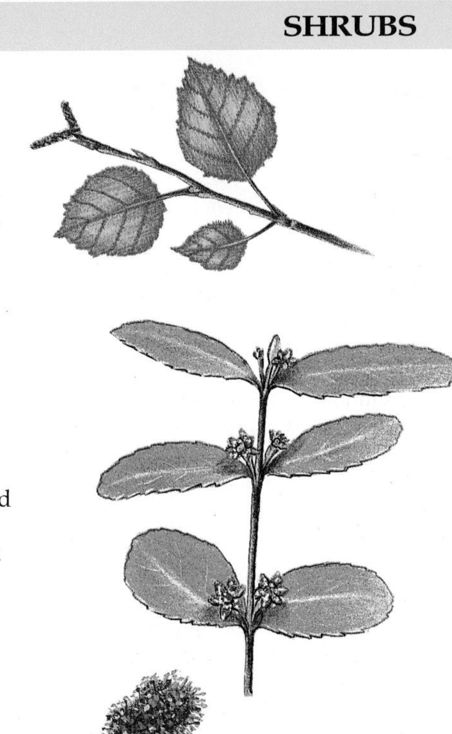

WATER BIRCH

Betula occidentalis
to 10 m (33 ft.)

A shrub or small tree found along the margins of lakes and streams. Its short trunk supports an irregular crown.

FALSEBOX

Pachistima myrsinites
to 1 m (3 ft.)

This low-growing evergreen shrub is found throughout BC in damp, coniferous forests. Its opposing, thick, leathery leaves (to 3 cm) are toothed and have slightly rolled edges. Reddish flowers bloom in tight clusters between leaves along the stem.

HARDHACK

Spiraea douglasii
to 1.5 m (5 ft.)

Found in damp, open areas at low to middle elevations in central and southern BC. Its narrow, oblong leaves are coarsely toothed along the upper half. The red-brown stems are especially visible during winter months. Showy pink flowers bloom in dense, cylindrical clusters.

BC WILDFLOWERS

What is a wildflower?

Wildflowers are soft-stemmed flowering plants, smaller than a tree or shrub, which grow anew each year. Some regenerate annually from the same rootstock (perennials), while others grow from seeds and last a single season (annuals). Most have flowering stems bearing colourful blossoms which ripen into fruits as the growing season progresses. Their flowering stem typically grows upright, but may be climbing, creeping or trailing. They range from weeds and reeds to roses and buttercups, and are found almost everywhere. From the cracks in city sidewalks, to mountain meadows, wildflowers are abundant and widespread throughout BC.

The species in this section have been grouped according to colour rather than family in order to facilitate field identification. The colour groups used are:

- White;
- Yellow and Green;
- Red, Pink and Orange; and
- Blue and Purple.

For those who are interested, the family name and taxonomic ordering of each species can be gleaned from the checklists in the back of the book.

How to identify wildflowers

After noting colour, examine the shape of the flower heads. Are they daisy-like, bell-shaped, or odd in appearance? How are they arranged on the plant? Do they occur singly, or in rounded or elongated clusters? Are the flower heads upright or drooping? Pay close attention to the leaves and how they are arranged on the stem. (See page 84 for leaf characteristics.) Refer to the illustrations and text to confirm its size, habitat and blooming period.

N.B. — The blooming periods of flowers can vary depending on latitude, elevation and the weather. The dates given are merely meant to serve as general guidelines.

Remember that flowers are wildlife and should be treated as such. Many species have been seriously depleted owing to loss of habitat and over-picking. In many areas, once abundant species are now rare. Bring along a sketchbook and camera and record the flowers you see, without picking them. This will help ensure there are more blossoms for you and others to enjoy next year.

The following drawings illustrate the different possible arrangements of multiple flowerheads on a stem.

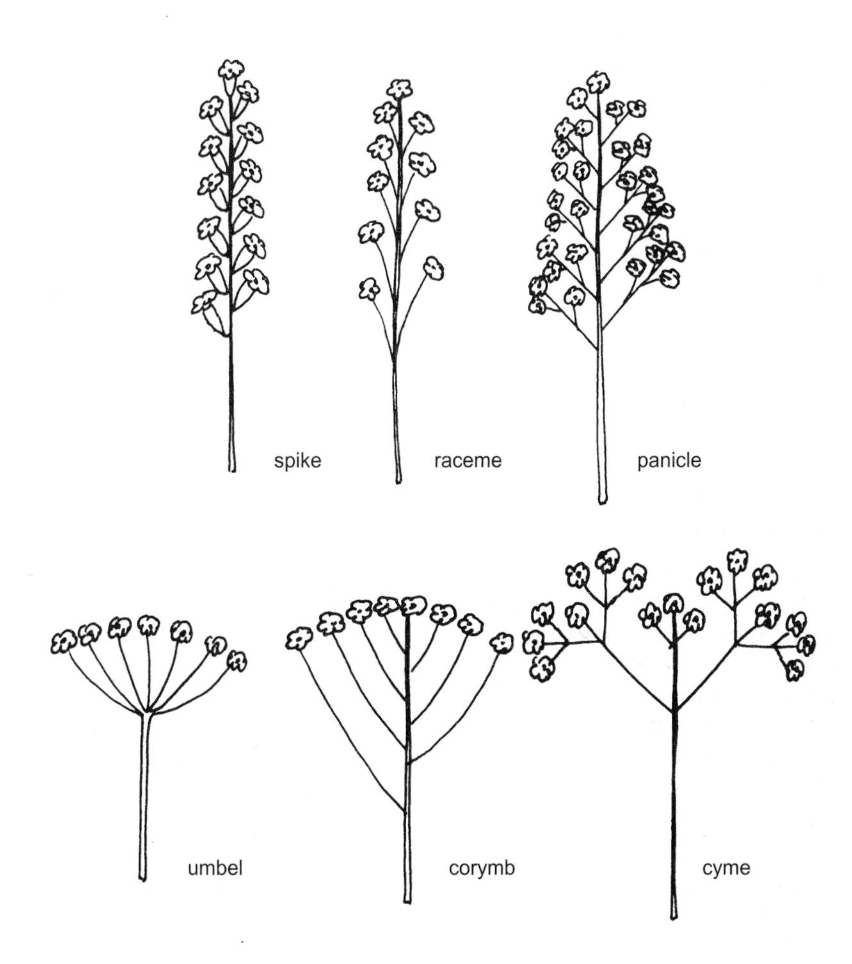

WHITE FLOWERS

STAR-FLOWERED SOLOMON'S SEAL

Smilacina trifolia
to 60 cm (2 ft.)

Found in moist, wooded areas and meadows throughout BC. Its alternate, lance-shaped leaves (to 12 cm) point upward. This plant is named for its star-like, creamy flowers which grow in a small cluster at the stem tip. Flowers bloom from April–June.

FALSE ASPHODEL

Tofieldia glutinosa
to 45 cm (18")

Found in wet woods, ditches and marshy areas. The two to four grass-like basal leaves are slender and are half the stem in length. A single, sticky-hairy stem supports a terminal cluster of small, white flowers that bloom in July–August. Stamens normally project beyond the petal margin and have conspicuous, purplish anthers. The flowers are replaced by conspicuous red capsules in autumn.

RED AND WHITE BANEBERRY

Actaea rubra
to 1 m (3 ft.)

This perennial herb is far more conspicuous when in fruit than in flower. Its large, compound leaves are deeply saw-toothed and have many pointed leaflets. The long, leafy stems support dense, conical crowns of tiny, delicate, white flowers that bloom from April–June. In summer the flowers are replaced by red or white, poisonous berries. Common in moist forests throughout BC.

WESTERN ANEMONE

Anemone occidentalis
to 60 cm (2 ft.)

Found in alpine meadows at middle to upper elevations. Its hairy leaves occur in a basal cluster and a single stem cluster. Its solitary, creamy flower blooms at the tip of its hairy stem shortly after the snow has melted. The flower is replaced by a "mop" of fluffy seeds.

GRASS OF PARNASSUS

Parnassia fimbrata
to 30 cm (12")

Found in dense colonies in wet areas and along streams. A cluster of glossy, kidney-shaped leaves spread out from the plant base. Each stem supports a solitary, star-shaped flower and has a single, stalkless leaf between its middle and base. The flower has lightly-veined petals and is fringed with fine hairs near the base. Blooms in August–September.

WHITE CLOVER

Trifolium repens
to 30 cm (12")

This introduced plant is common in fields, lawns and waste areas. Its long-stemmed, dark green leaves have three oval leaflets and grow densely along creeping, mat-forming stems. Rounded, white flowers bloom from April–September. An excellent nectar producer, it is a favourite of bees. Red and Pink Clover (*T. pratense* and *T. hybridium* respectively) are also common in the province.

COW PARSNIP

Heracleum lanatum
to 2 m (6 ft.)

This large, conspicuous plant is very common in moist fields and woods. Large, deeply-lobed leaves grow along the length of its thick, hollow stem. Dense, flattened clusters of creamy white flowers bloom between May–August, depending on location. Though non-poisonous, it resembles similar plants, like the Water Hemlock, which are deadly.

ARROW-LEAVED COLTSFOOT

Petasites sagittatus
to 30 cm (12")

Common and widespread in moist woodlands and boggy areas. Its large, arrow-shaped basal leaves (to 25 cm) are grey-green above, white and hairy below. Tiny, white flowers bloom in dense terminal clusters from March–June. These are succeeded by tufts of cottony seeds which resemble small cotton balls. A purple coltsfoot (*P. speciosa*) also occurs in BC.

BUNCHBERRY

Cornus canadensis
to 20 cm (8")

A mat-forming herb very common in moist woods and bogs throughout the province. Stems arise from a creeping rootstock which runs underground. Each plant has a whorl of four to seven oval, parallel-veined leaves. The four white, petal-like lobes of the flower are actually bracts which surround a small cluster of greenish-yellow flowers. Blooms in May–June. Flowers are succeeded by tight clusters of bright red berries.

BUCK-BEAN

Menyanthes trifoliata
to 20 cm (8")

This semi-aquatic plant grows in shallow water in ditches and boggy areas. The thick, compound leaves have three rounded, toothless leaflets. Its tubular, white flowers have glistening hairs on their upper surface and a feathery appearance. Flowers and leaves arise from a thick, creeping stem. Blooms in May–June.

PHLOX

Phlox spp.
to 45 cm (18")

This group of mat-forming plants occur throughout the province on dry soils. The plant can be identified as a green "cushion" sprinkled with small, colourful, five-lobed, yellow-centred flowers, which range in colour from pink and lavender to yellow and white. Several variants may be found within a small area. Blooms from March–August.

COMMON PLANTAIN

Plantago major
to 50 cm

An introduced species very common in lawns, gardens and waste areas throughout the province. Large, tough, basal leaves are finely toothed with deep, longitudinal veins. Tiny, greenish flowers bloom in a slender spike. Four other similar species of plantain are found in BC.

RATTLESNAKE PLANTAIN

Goodyera oblongifolia
to 36 cm (14")

Found in dry areas in mossy, coniferous forests. Its leaves grow in a basal cluster and are easily identified by their snakeskin-like markings. Whitish flowers bloom in a loose cluster at the stem tip in summer. The juice from crushed leaves apparently soothes cuts and bruises.

NORTHERN BEDSTRAW

Galium boreale
to 60 cm (2 ft.)

Very common in moist woods, meadows and along roadsides throughout BC. Its narrow leaves grow in whorls of four along slender, four-sided stems. Dense clusters of tiny, cross-shaped, white flowers bloom in terminal clusters in July–August. These abundant, fragrant plants were once used as mattress stuffing. Over half a dozen similar species of bedstraw are found in BC.

COMMON YARROW

Achillea millefolium
to 60 cm (2 ft.)

This aromatic herb is common in ditches, fields and waste areas. The unusual, fern-like leaves are a good field mark. Its long, un-branched stem supports dense clusters of round, yellow-centred, daisy-like flowers. Each flower has four to six white (occasionally pinkish) rays. Blooms from June–August.

PEARLY EVERLASTING

Anaphalis margaritacea
to 60 cm (2 ft.)

Widespread throughout BC in a variety of habitats. Its alternate, lance-shaped stem leaves are green above and woolly-white below. Pearly flowers bloom in flat-topped clusters in summer and can last until late autumn.

WHITE MOSS HEATHER

Cassiope mertensiana
to 30 cm (1 ft.)

This mat-forming plant is very common in alpine and subalpine regions. Tiny, scale-like leaves are arranged in four rows and overlap along its twigs. Snowy, bell-shaped flowers bloom near the stem tips and have reddish sepals at their base.

UNIFLORA

Clintonia uniflora
to 20 cm (8")

This widespread flower is common in moist forests at middle mountain elevations. The long, shiny leaves (to 20 cm) that grow in a basal rosette are a good field mark. A slender flower stem supports a single, large, white, cup-shaped flower. Flowers are followed by distinctive steel-blue berries.

MOUNTAIN DAISY

Erigeron peregrinus
to 60 cm (2 ft.)

Found on dry slopes and rocky areas at middle to high elevations. Its lance-shaped leaves are velvety and decrease in size from plant base to tip. Flowers have numerous, thin, white or lavender rays (50+) and yellowish centres. Over 20 similar species are found in BC.

COTTON GRASS

Eriophorum chamissonis
to 50 cm (20")

Found in bogs and wet areas at low to middle elevations. Its narrow leaves are short, grass-like and primarily basal. The slender, springy stem supports a distinctive white, cottony head. It often grows in thick colonies, covering entire meadows.

WILD STRAWBERRY

Fragaria virginiana
to 15 cm (6")

This mat-forming plant is found in open areas and forest margins throughout the province. Its basal leaves are bluish-green, coarsely toothed and divided into three leaflets. White flowers bloom in clusters on stems that are usually shorter than the surrounding leaves. The fruit is a juicy, sweet strawberry.

WILD LILY-OF-THE-VALLEY

Maianthemum dilatatum
to 25 cm (10")

Found in moist, mixed woods and forest clearings at low to middle elevations. Its two to three large, oval- to heart-shaped veiny leaves are a good field mark. White, lily-like flowers bloom in a slender terminal spike in May–June, and are succeeded by red berries.

INDIAN PIPE

Monotropa uniflora
to 25 cm (10")

These distinctive plants are found in shady areas in coniferous forests, primarily in the coastal region. The plant is waxy white or pinkish and darkens with age. White, bell-shaped flowers blend in with the waxy stem. Because the Indian Pipe lacks the green pigment chlorophyll necessary for photosynthesis, it obtains nourishment from decaying matter in the forest floor.

SAXIFRAGE

Saxifraga spp.
to 20 cm (8")

This large, diverse family of plants is represented by over 50 species in BC. The name means "rock-breaker" and many grow in rocky areas. Characteristics include leaves that are primarily basal and five-petalled flowers with 10 stamens and two styles. Many are less than 15 cm tall.

WESTERN TRILLIUM (WAKE ROBIN)

Trillium ovatum
to 60 cm (2 ft.)

Found in damp woods, it is one of the earliest spring flowers in southern BC. Distinguished at a glance as a white flower framed by a whorl of three large, net-veined leaves. The white flowers turn purplish as they age. Blooms from March–May.

YELLOW AND GREEN FLOWERS

COMMON CATTAIL

Typha latifolia
to 3 m (10 ft.)

This aquatic plant is common at low to middle elevations, in marshes, ditches and along lakes and rivers throughout the province. Familiar to most, it can be distinguished by its prominent, club-like sheath of greenish flower spikes atop a long stalk. The flowers ripen into brownish tufts of hairy seeds in late summer, giving the plant its characteristic appearance.

GLACIER LILY

Erythronium grandiflorum
to 40 cm (16")

Found in open meadows and moist woods in the foothills and mountains. Two large, slender leaves arise from the plant base. The naked flower stalk supports a large, bright yellow, nodding flower. As the plant matures, the pointed petals gently fold back to expose the pistil and stamens. Blooms from March–June (depending on elevation). One of the first flowers to bloom in spring, it often appears before the snow has completely melted.

DEATH CAMAS

Zygadenus elegans
to 60 cm (2 ft.)

A foul-smelling flower common in damp meadows and open forests at middle to upper elevations. Its blue-green leaves are long and grass-like in appearance. Greenish lilies bloom in a loose terminal cluster from June–August. Their petals all have a greenish spot at their base. A highly poisonous plant, it has been responsible for a number of stock fatalities.

NORTHERN GREEN BOG ORCHID

Habenaria hyperborea
to 60 cm (2 ft.)

Found in bogs, marshes and damp woods throughout BC. Slender leaves clasp the stem, decreasing in size from base to tip. A narrow cluster of small green orchids are crowded near the tip of the stem. Flowers are distinguished by a curved spur which tapers to a point. It blooms from June–August. A dozen similar species occur in BC.

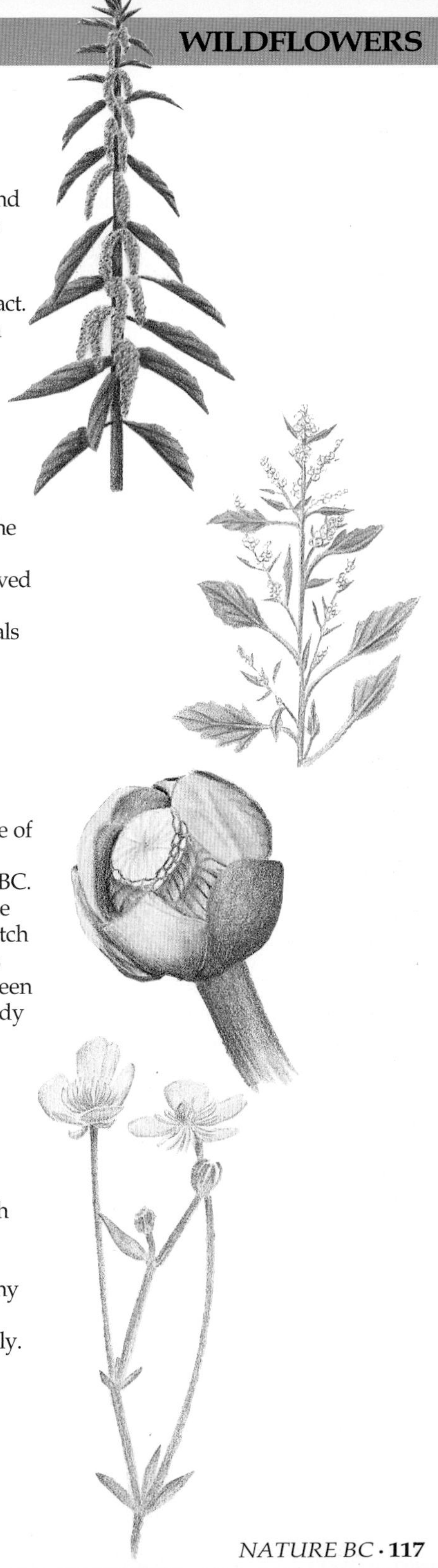

COMMON NETTLE
Urtica dioica
to 3 m (10 ft.)

Common in shady thickets, meadows and waste areas throughout the province. Its coarsely saw-toothed, opposing leaves have sharp prickles that eject an acidic stinging substance (formic acid) on contact. Drooping spikes of green flowers bloom June–August.

LAMB'S QUARTERS
Chenopodium album
to 1 m (3 ft.)

This familiar, introduced weed is widespread throughout the province. The oval leaves are covered with a mealy substance. It is distinguished by its grooved stalk, numerous branching stems and dense foliage. Greenish flowers lack petals and resemble tiny cauliflowers. Blooms from June–August.

YELLOW POND LILY
Nuphar lutea
to 20 cm (8")

An aquatic plant. Found on the surface of sloughs, ponds and slow-moving streams at low elevations throughout BC. Its buoyant, leathery leaves float on the surface and have a deep, V-shaped notch at their base. A bright yellow, bulbous flower blooms among the leaves between June–July. Roots are anchored in muddy bottoms of ponds and streams.

BUTTERCUP
Ranunculus spp.
to 1 m (3 ft.)

BC is home to over 30 species of this very common flower group. Though there is a wide variance in the habitat, shape and size of members, all have alternate leaves and brilliant yellow, shiny petals with a small scale near the base. Blooming periods range from March–July.

WILD MUSTARD
Brassica kaber
to 1 m (3 ft.)

An introduced weed very common in fields, ditches and waste areas. Its alternate leaves are slender and irregularly toothed. The hairy stem supports dense clusters of cross-shaped yellow flowers which bloom in May–June. Each flower has four broad yellow petals and four green sepals.

YELLOW DRYAD
Dryas drummondi
to 25 cm (10")

Common on rocky soil in the foothills and mountain regions. The leathery leaves are shiny green above, woolly-white below. Its leafless, hairy stem rises from a dense mat of low-growing leaves and supports a single, nodding, yellow flower. Note the hairy leaves (sepals) enclosing the flower at its base. Blooms from June–August. The similar White Dryad (*D. octopetala*) is common in alpine regions.

YELLOW LOCOWEED
Oxytropis campestris
to 40 cm (16")

Common in dry and rocky soils, open woodlands and meadows. Its grey-green leaves have 7–20 leaflets and grow upward from the plant base. Pale yellow flowers are loosely clustered in a terminal spike. It often grows in thick clusters. Blooms May–July. Six similar species occur in BC, many of which, when eaten, appear to cause mental disturbances in livestock.

YELLOW TOAD FLAX (BUTTER AND EGGS)

Linaria vulgaris
to 60 cm (2 ft.)

An introduced weed common in fields and waste areas at lower elevations throughout BC. The grey-green leaves are narrow, stalkless and grow along the length of the stem. Yellow flowers bloom in long, terminal clusters; each has a long, tapered spur and a prominent orange pouch on its lower lip. Blooms in June–July.

HEART-LEAVED ARNICA

Arnica cordifolia
to 60 cm (2 ft.)

Widespread throughout BC at low to middle elevations. Its opposing leaves are heart-shaped, long-stemmed and sharply serrated. The coarse stem supports a bright yellow, daisy-like flower with wide-spreading petals. Related to a dozen similar BC species. Blooms from June–August.

COMMON DANDELION

Taraxacum officinale
to 30 cm (12")

Abundant in open and grassy areas, this introduced plant is one of the most widespread plants in the province. A stemless plant, its cut-toothed leaves and flowering stalk arise from a fleshy taproot. Its bright yellow flowers bloom frequently throughout the growing season. Tufts of whitish, hairy seeds succeed the flowers, and are dispersed by the wind. The leaves are commonly used in salads, and the blossoms for wine-making.

CANADA GOLDENROD

Solidago canadensis
to 1 m (3 ft.)

Common in dense colonies on the margins of forests, thickets and roadsides at lower elevations. Its long leaves are lance-shaped, toothed and deeply veined. Clusters of yellow, daisy-like flowers are borne along spreading, recurved branches. Blooms in midsummer. A number of similar species are found in BC.

INDIAN HELLEBORE

Veratrum viride
to 2 m (7 ft.)

Common in moist to wet areas in forests and alpine meadows. Its large, broad leaves (to 30 cm) are prominently veined and "tropical" in appearance. Inconspicuous greenish, star-shaped flowers bloom in large drooping spikes between May–August (depending on elevation). Roots contain a highly toxic poison.

LARGE-LEAVED AVENS

Geum macrophyllum
to 1 m (3 ft.)

Common in moist soils in woods, meadows and clearings throughout BC. Its large, ragged, basal leaves (to 30 cm) have three lobes with a large terminal segment; stem leaves are rounded and deeply triple-lobed. Flowers bloom singly or in small clusters from May–July. Six similar species are found in BC.

WOOLLY SUNFLOWER

Eriophyllum lanatum
to 30 cm (12")

Found on dry soils and rocky ledges in exposed areas in southern BC. This plant is named for its woolly leaves; stem leaves have five to seven lobes while lower leaves are whole. Yellow-centred, yellow flower has seven to twelve broad petals. Blooms from May–August.

SPRING SUNFLOWER (BALSAMROOT)

Balsamorhiza sagittata
to 60 cm (2 ft.)

Found in dry, open areas and on open slopes at low and middle elevations. The large, arrow-shaped basal leaves (to 30 cm) grow densely together. Numerous slender stems arising from the base support a single, brilliant, yellow ray-flower. Blooms in May. Its oily root was an important food source to Indians.

YELLOW VIOLET

Viola glabella
to 25 cm (10")

Found in moist forests, clearings and near streams at low to middle elevations throughout the province. Its heart-shaped leaves have sharply pointed tips and branch near the stem tip. The yellow flower has conspicuous dark veins on its petals. Several other species of yellow violet are found in BC, as well as some that are mauve, white or blue.

OVAL-LEAF ALUMROOT

Heuchera cylindrica
to 50 cm (20")

Widespread throughout southern BC, on exposed rocky soils at low elevations. Its oval, thick, basal leaves are hairy and sticky. Small, yellow flowers bloom in terminal spikes from May–August. Several similar species of yellow and white alumroots are found in BC.

YELLOW MONKEY FLOWER

Mimulus guttatas
to 60 cm (2 ft.)

Common in wet areas at various elevations throughout BC. Oval leaves are coarsely toothed; lower leaves are stalked, upper ones are clasping. Trumpet-shaped, yellow flowers have dark-spotted, hairy throats. Blooms in loose terminal clusters from May–August.

STONECROP

Sedum spp.
to 25 cm (10")

This family of low-growing plants are common on dry, rocky soils throughout BC. Narrow, fleshy, alternate leaves grow closely together with most near the base. Bright, star-like, yellow to purple flowers bloom in dense terminal clusters during May–June.

RED, PINK AND ORANGE FLOWERS

NODDING ONION

Allium cernuum
to 50 cm (20")

Found in open woodlands and moist meadows in central and southern BC. The leaves are grass-like and grow upward from the plant base. Its slender flowering stalk supports a large, nodding cluster of pinkish, bulbous flowers. The entire plant has an onion-like odour. Blooms from May–July.

FIREWEED

Epilobium angustifolium
to 2 m (7 ft.)

Very common in open woodlands, clearings and burned-out areas, it is the floral emblem of the Yukon Territory. Alternate, narrow, willow-like leaves grow along the length of the stem. Its long, conical spike of bright pink, four-petalled flowers is unmistakable. It often grows in dense colonies. Blooms from June–August.

COMMON PINK WINTERGREEN

Pyrola asarifolia
to 40 cm (15")

Found in moist woods and swampy areas throughout BC. The glossy, heart-shaped basal leaves are green above, purplish below. Its slender, reddish flowering stem has a long, terminal cluster of up to 20 drooping, pink flowers. Fragrant, bell-shaped flowers bloom from June–August. At least nine similar species of wintergreen occur in BC.

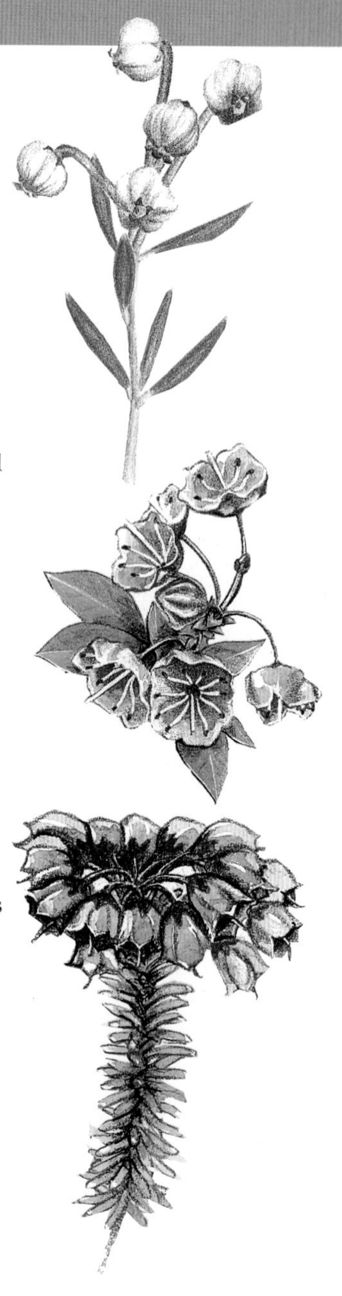

BOG ROSEMARY

Andromeda polifolia (Heath Family)
to 40 cm (16")

Common in swamps and bogs in wooded areas. Shiny, slender leaves are leathery and grow upward along the length of the stem. Pinkish, urn-shaped flowers bloom in nodding clusters between May–June.

SWAMP-LAUREL

Kalmia polifolia
to 50 cm (20")

This shrubby flower is found in bogs and wet meadows. Its narrow, opposing leaves have whitish undersides and grow along the length of the branching stem. The reddish-purple flowers are noted for their "sprung" stamens which are loaded into petal pouches. When disturbed by an insect, the stamens spring forth and dust the intruder with pollen.

RED HEATHER

Phyllodoce empetriformis
to 30 cm (12")

This small, mat-forming shrub is common at upper elevations in the mountains. Its alternate, evergreen leaves are needle-like and grooved on both surfaces. Bell-shaped pinkish flowers bloom in nodding terminal clusters in June–July. It often grows in close association with similar species of white and yellow heather.

SHOOTING STAR

Dodecatheon spp.
to 30 cm (12")

Common on moist soil in meadows, fields and open woodlands. Narrow leaves are widest near their tip and grow upward from the plant base. A small cluster of beautiful, red-purple flowers bloom at the tip of the reddish flowering stem. The flower petals arch backward gracefully to expose the yellow stamen tube. Blooms from March–May. About half a dozen similar species occur in BC.

INDIAN PAINTBRUSH

Castilleja spp.
to 60 cm (2 ft.)

Common and widespread in woodlands and meadows, BC is home to several species of paintbrush. Alternate leaves are narrow and grow along the entire stem length. The brush-like spike atop the stem is composed of colourful bracts surrounding inconspicuous, green-yellow flowers. Bract colour ranges from red and orange to yellow and white. Indian Paintbrush blooms from June–August.

ELEPHANT'S HEAD

Pedicularis groenlandica
to 50 cm (20")

Common in wet meadows and marshes in the foothills and mountain regions. Dark green leaves are fern-like and heavily dissected. Leafy stems support long clusters of red-purple flowers which resemble an elephant's head and trunk. Blooms from June–August.

PINK PUSSYTOES

Antennaria spp.
to 30 cm (12")

Common in dry meadows and open woodlands. Its leaves, stem and flowers have a woolly appearance. The shortish, flowering stalk bears a terminal cluster of furry, pinkish or white flowers which bloom May–August.

CANADA THISTLE

Cirsium arvense
to 1 m (3 ft.)

A very common introduced weed found in ditches and fields throughout the province. Its dark green leaves are scalloped and have prickly margins. The branching stem supports several small clusters of woolly, pinkish-mauve (occasionally white) flowers. Blooms from June–August. Over half a dozen similar species are found in BC.

RED COLUMBINE

Aquileja formosa
to 1 m (3 ft.)

Found on well-drained soils in open forests, meadows and glades. Its leaves are mostly basal and divided into three leaflets. The stunning, red-orange flower head with tall spurs is unmistakable. An important source of food for hummingbirds and butterflies, it blooms from May–August. Similar species of blue and yellow columbines are also found in BC.

PIPSISSEWA

Chimaphila umbellata
to 25 cm (10")

Found in cool, moist, coniferous forests throughout BC. Its leathery, evergreen leaves are coarsely toothed and whorled around the stem. Small, saucer-shaped, waxy, pink flowers (3–10) bloom in a nodding cluster at the stem tip in May–June. Once used as a tea substitute by early settlers.

RED MONKEY FLOWER

Mimulus lewisii
to 60 cm (2 ft.)

Found in or near water at middle to high mountain elevations. Opposing leaves (to 10 cm) are waxy, prominently veined, and occur along the entire stem length. Pairs of bright, pink-red, trumpet-shaped "snapdragons" bloom at the stem tip in summer. The similar Yellow Monkey Flower *(Mimulus guttatus)* is also found in BC.

TIGER LILY

Lilium columbianum
to 1 m (3 ft.)

Found on damp soils in meadows and open woodlands. Small, narrow leaves are arranged in whorls along the stem. The striking, red-orange flower head is speckled with dark spots and blooms in clusters of up to nine from May–July. Anthers protrude far beyond the flower margin.

TWISTED STALK

Streptopus roseus
to 1 m (3 ft.)

Common in moist, open forests throughout the province. The unbranching stem is densely covered with alternate, oval leaves. Small, reddish-pink, bell-shaped flowers have flared, white tips. It blooms in June–July. This plant is named for its thin flower stalks, which are sharply twisted.

BLUE AND PURPLE FLOWERS

DOUGLAS ASTER

Aster douglasii
to 1 m (3 ft.)

This species is representative of the more than 25 asters found in BC. Found along well-drained roadsides and in open forests, it is identified at a glance by its showy, bluish-purple flowers. The coarse leaves are stalkless and grow along the length of its stout stems. Its flowers have numerous, thin rays (10–50) and yellowish centres. Blooms in August–September.

ARCTIC LUPINE

Lupinus arcticus
to 60 cm (2 ft.)

Common in fields, on roadsides and in open areas throughout BC. The leaves consist of six to eight very narrow leaflets which radiate like wheel spokes from a central axis. Bluish-purple flowers bloom in long, terminal clusters from June–August.

VENUS' SLIPPER

Calypso bulbosa
to 20 cm (8")

This beautiful orchid is commonly found in dry, mossy woodlands. A single, broad, pointed leaf grows at the plant base. The striking, pinkish flower has an inflated, slipper-like lower lip which often has a white outer edge; the inner surface is streaked and dark-spotted and features rows of golden yellow hairs. One of our earliest blooming orchids, it is often found in dense colonies. Venus' Slipper blooms from April–June.

STICKY PURPLE GERANIUM

Geranium viscosissimum
to 60 cm (2 ft.)

Common in meadows, fields and open woodlands. Its dark green leaves have long stalks and are divided into five to seven coarsely-toothed lobes. Both the leaf stalks and flowering stem are sticky to the touch; this feature is believed to prevent pollen theft by crawling insects. Showy, purple-pink, veined flowers are an excellent field mark. Blooms from May–July.

EARLY BLUE VIOLET

Viola adunca
to 10 cm (4")

Very common in moist woods and meadows throughout the province. Its long-stalked basal leaves are oval or heart-shaped. The leaves and flowers arise from a fleshy rootstock on stems which are slightly hairy. Small, five-petalled, blue-violet flowers bloom in April–May. The inner edges of the petals and the style are hairy. Yellow and white violets also occur in BC.

NORTHERN GENTIAN

Gentianella amarella
to 50 cm (20")

Common in moist fields, thickets and along streambanks. Its light green leaves are oblong and grow along the entire stem length. A terminal cluster of fringed, tubular flowers blooms from June–September. Flowers are typically purplish-blue, but may sometimes be whitish. About a dozen gentians are found in BC.

ALPINE FORGET-ME-NOT

Myosotis alpestris
to 30 cm (12")

This familiar alpine flower is common in moist mountain meadows. The narrow leaves have a prominent central vein and are stalked near the base of the plant, stalkless near the top. Distinguished at a glance by its cluster of beautiful, yellow-centred, mauve flowers. Blooms from June–August.

BEARD TONGUE

Pentstemon spp.
to 30 cm (12")

A dozen of these beautiful herbs are found on dry and rocky soils throughout BC. The short-stalked leaves are oval to lance-shaped and tend to clasp the plant near the stem tip. Bright, bluish-purple, tubular flowers bloom in a loose terminal cluster from May–July. In most, the throat and lower lip of the flower is very hairy. Often found growing in clumps.

BLUEBELL (HAREBELL)

Campanula rotundifolia
to 50 cm (20")

Very common on drier soils at low to middle elevations throughout the province. Basal leaves are rounded or heart-shaped and usually wither at the onset of flowering. Narrow stem leaves persist. Grass-like, flowering stems terminate in clusters of nodding, bell-shaped flowers, typically mauve, but blue and white variants are not uncommon. Often grows in dense clumps. Blooms from June–September.

SHOWY JACOB'S LADDER

Polemonium pulcherrimum
to 30 cm (12")

Common on sandy and rocky soils in open areas at low to high elevations. This plant is named for its leaves, which have a ladder-like arrangement of 10–25 leaflets, and have a skunky odour when crushed. Blue, bell-shaped flowers bloom in crowded terminal clusters during June–July.

PHACELIA

Phacelia linearis
to 50 cm (20")

Found in dry areas at lower elevations in southern BC. Alternate leaves are linear near the base, and triple-lobed on the upper part of the plant. Lavender, veined flowers bloom in small clusters from April–August. White and dark blue variants also exist.

CAMAS

Camassia quamash
to 60 cm (2 ft.)

Common in southern BC, especially in the Gulf Islands region. The grass-like leaves grow upward from the plant base. Bluish-purple flowers bloom in crowded terminal clusters of 10–30 between April–June. White variants also exist.

MILKWEED

Ascelpias speciosa
to 1.2 m (4 ft.)

Found on dry soils in waste areas and ditches in southern BC. Its large, fleshy leaves (to 15 cm) are finely haired. Both the leaves and stem secrete a sticky fluid to protect the flowers from crawling insects. Purplish, horned flowers bloom in tight clusters in July–August. In autumn, long seed pods split open to release thousands of long-plumed seeds.

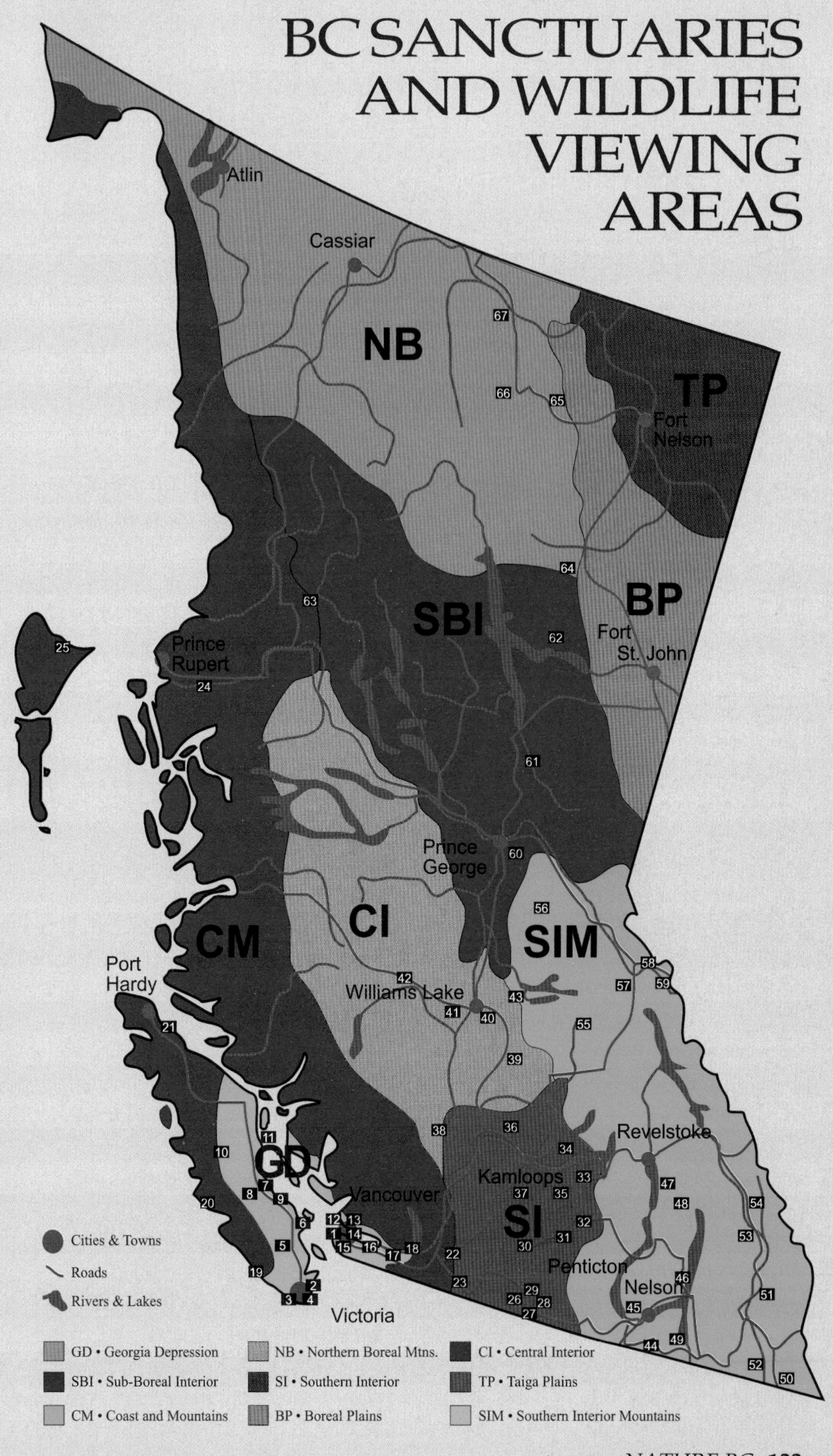
BC SANCTUARIES AND WILDLIFE VIEWING AREAS
Atlin
Cassiar
NB
TP
Fort Nelson
SBI
BP
Fort St. John
Prince Rupert
Prince George
CI
CM
SIM
Port Hardy
Williams Lake
GD
Vancouver
Kamloops
SI
Revelstoke
Penticton
Nelson
Victoria
1 2 3 4 5 6 7 8 9 10 11 12 13 14 15 16 17 18 19 20 21 22 23 24 25 26 27 28 29 30 31 32 33 34 35 36 37 38 39 40 41 42 43 44 45 46 47 48 49 50 51 52 53 54 55 56 57 58 59 60 61 62 63 64 65 66 67
Cities & Towns
Roads
Rivers & Lakes
GD • Georgia Depression
NB • Northern Boreal Mtns.
CI • Central Interior
SBI • Sub-Boreal Interior
SI • Southern Interior
TP • Taiga Plains
CM • Coast and Mountains
BP • Boreal Plains
SIM • Southern Interior Mountains

Wildlife Viewing Areas

Site #	Site Name	Eco province	Highlights
1	Bellhouse Prov. Park/Active Pass	GD	Seabirds, Eagles, Sea Lions, Killer Whales (a)
2	Sidney Spit Prov. Marine Park	GD	Fallow Deer, Herons, Eagles, Seabirds
3	Goldstream Prov. Park	GD	Spawning Salmon
4	Swan Lake Nature Sanctuary	GD	Excellent Birdwatching
5	Somenos Marsh	GD	Waterfowl, Shorebirds (a)
6	Nanaimo Harbour	GD	Sea Lions, Eagles, Seabirds
7	Courtenay River Estuary	GD	Trumpeter Swans (a), Waterfowl, Shorebirds (b)
8	Stamp Falls Prov. Park	GD	Spawning Salmon
9	Parksville/Qualicum Beach	GD	Black Brant (a), Brant Festival (b) (mid-Apr.), Waterfowl (c)
10	Strathcona Prov. Park	GD	Elk, Trumpeter Swans
11	Mitlenatch Island Prov. Park	GD	Gull Colony, Cormorants, Oystercatchers
12	Iona Beach Regional Park	GD	Shorebirds, Songbirds, Raptors
13	Reifel Migratory Bird Sanctuary	GD	Estuarine Marsh, 230 Bird Species
14	Boundary Bay	GD	Waterfowl, Shorebirds, Raptors
15	Serpentine Wildlife Area	GD	Waterfowl, Shorebirds, Raptors
16	Burnaby Lake Regional Park	GD	Songbirds, Waterfowl, Bats
17	Pitt-Addington WMA*	GD	Waterfowl, Swans, Cranes, Raptors
18	Harrison River/Kilby Prov. Park	GD	Eagles, Herons, Waterfowl, Spawning Salmon (a)
19	French Beach Prov. Park	CM	Gray Whales (a), Seabirds, Intertidal Fauna
20	Pacific Rim National Park	CM	Gray Whales (a), Shorebirds (b), Intertidal Fauna
21	Blackfish Sound/Johnstone Strait	CM	Killer Whales, Eagles, Porpoises
22	Coquihalla Canyon Prov. Park	CM	Spawning Steelhead Trout
23	Manning Prov. Park	CM	Marmots(a), Songbirds, Ground Squirrels (a)
24	Lower Skeena River	CM	Eulachon, Sea Lions, Seals, Eagles
25	Delkatla Slough	CM	Cranes, Shorebirds, Waterfowl, Eagles
26	Hedley-Keremeos Cliffs	SI	Mountain Goats
27	Osoyoos Oxbows	SI	Bobolinks (a), Turtles (b), Ospreys (c)
28	Vaseux Lake	SI	Bighorn Sheep, Waterfowl, Birdwatching, Reptiles (a)
29	Okanagan Falls Prov. Park	SI	Bats, Nighthawks, Swallows (a)
30	Peachland Creek	SI	Spawning Kokanee
31	Mission Creek Reg. Park	SI	Spawning Kokanee
32	Kalamalka Lake Prov. Park	SI	Rattlesnakes (a)†, Marmots (a), Birdwatching
33	Salmon Arm Bay	SI	Western Grebes (a), Shorebirds(b), Waterfowl

Viewing Seasons

J	F	M	A	M	J	J	A	S	O	N	D
•	•	•	•	•	•a	•a	•a	•a	•	•	•
					•	•	•	•			
									•	•	
•	•	•	•	•	•	•	•	•	•	•	•
•	•	•	•a	•a	•	•	•	•	•	•	•
•	•	•	•								•
•a	•a	•a	•ab	•b	•	•	•	•	•	•a	•a
						•	•	•	•		
		a	abc	c	c	c	c	c	c		
•	•	•	•								•
					•	•	•	•			
•	•	•	•	•	•	•	•	•	•	•	•
•	•	•	•	•	•	•	•	•	•	•	•
•	•	•	•	•	•	•	•	•	•	•	•
•	•	•	•	•	•	•	•	•	•	•	•
•	•	•	•	•	•	•	•	•	•	•	•
•	•	•	•	•	•	•	•	•	•	•	•
•	•								•a	•a	•
•	•	•a	•a	•	•	•	•	•	•	•	•
•	•	•a	•ab	•b	•	•	•	•	•	•	•
					•	•	•	•			
					•	•					
			•	•a	•a	•a	•a	•	•		
		•									
•	•	•	•	•	•	•	•	•	•	•	•
•	•	•	•	•	•	•	•	•	•	•	•
			abc	abc	abc	bc	bc	bc	c		
•	•	•	•	•a	•a	•a	•a	•a	•	•	•
				•	•	•a	•a	•			
								•	•		
								•	•		
•	•	•	•	•a	•a	•a	•a	•a	•	•	•
•	•	•b	•ab	•ab	•ab	•ab	•ab	•ab	•ab	•b	•

Site #	Site Name	Eco province	Highlights
34	Adams River/Haig Brown Prov. Park	SI	Spawning Sockeye Salmon
35	South Thompson River	SI	Ospreys (a), Swans (b), Waterfowl (b), Bighorn Sheep
36	Tranquille/Dewdrop WMA*	SI	Waterfowl (a), Bighorn Sheep, Mule Deer (b)
37	Nicola Valley Corridor	SI	Owls, Hawks, Coyotes, Cranes (a)
38	Seton Lake	CI	Mountain Goats
39	100 Mile Marsh	CI	Waterfowl, Birdwatching
40	Scout Island	CI	Waterfowl (a), Foxes (b)
41	Junction WMA*	CI	Calif. Bighorn Sheep, Long-Billed Curlews (a), Grouse (b)
42	Chilanko Marsh WMA*	CI	Waterfowl, Beavers, Muskrats
43	Horsefly River	CI	Spawning Sockeye Salmon
44	Pend D'Oreille Valley	SIM	White-Tailed Deer (a), Mule Deer (b)
45	Lower Arrow Lake/Syringa Crk. Park	SIM	Bighorn Sheep (a), Deer (b), Black Bears (c)
46	Kokanee Creek Prov. Park	SIM	Spawning Kokanee (a), Birdwatching
47	Hill Creek	SIM	Spawning Kokanee
48	Gerrard	SIM	Spawning Rainbow Trout (a), Kokanee (b)
49	Creston Valley WMA*	SIM	Excellent Birdwatching, 240 Bird Species
50	Elko	SIM	Bighorn Sheep, Mountain Goats
51	Premier Lake Prov. Park	SIM	Spawning Rainbow Trout
52	Kikomun Creek	SIM	Turtles (a), (Elk, Deer) (b), Spawning Kokanee (c)
53	Columbia Wetlands	SIM	Elk, Deer, Moose, Waterfowl, Raptors
54	Kootenay National Park	SIM	Elk, Bighorn Sheep, Wolves, Mountain Goats
55	Wells Gray Prov. Park	SIM	Black Bears (a), Moose (b), Chinook Salmon (c)
56	Bowron Lake Prov. Park	SIM	Moose, Beavers, Ospreys, Waterfowl
57	Cranberry Marsh	SIM	Waterfowl, Raptors, Muskrat
58	Rearguard Falls Prov. Park	SIM	Spawning Chinook Salmon
59	Mt. Robson Prov. Park (Moose Marsh)	SIM	Moose (a), Muskrats (b), Birdwatching (b)
60	Tabor Mountain	SBI	Moose, Wolves, Raptors
61	Crooked River	SBI	Trumpeter Swans, Waterfowl, Moose
62	Dunlevy Creek	SBI	Stone Sheep (a), Elk (b), Golden Eagles (c)
63	Babine River	SBI	Spawning Sockeye, Eagles
64	Pink Mountain	NB	Caribou, Moose, Ptarmigan, Wolves
65	Stone Mountain Prov. Park	NB	Caribou, Moose
66	Muncho Lake Prov. Park	NB	Stone Sheep (a), Caribou, Moose
67	Liard River Hotsprings Prov. Park	NB	Moose (a), Waterfowl (b), Lake Chub

** Wildlife Management Area*

† Warning: Do not approach rattlesnakes; be careful where you step or put your hands.

The map on page 133 and this chart are reproduced with the permission of the BC Ministry of Environment.

Viewing Seasons

J	F	M	A	M	J	J	A	S	O	N	D
								•	•		
•b	•b	•b	•b	•ab	•a	•a	•a	•	•b	•b	•b
•	•	•ab	•ab	•ab	•	•	•	•a	•a	•a	•
•	•	•	•a	•	•	•	•	•a	•	•	•
•	•	•	•	•	•	•	•	•	•	•	•
			•	•	•	•	•	•	•		
			a	a	ab	ab	ab	ab	a		
			•	•a	•a	•a	•	•b	•b	•b	
			•	•	•	•	•	•	•		
							•	•			
a	a	a	a	b	b						
ab	ab	ab	ab	abc	abc	ab	a	a	a	a	a
				•	•	•	•a	•a	•		
								•			
				a				b			
			•	•	•	•	•	•	•		
•	•	•	•	•	•	•	•	•	•	•	•
				•	•						
	b	b	b			a	a	c	c		
•	•	•	•	•	•	•	•	•	•	•	•
•	•	•	•	•	•	•	•	•	•	•	•
b	b	b	b	a	a		bc	bc	ab	b	b
				•	•	•	•	•	•		
			•	•	•	•	•	•			
							•	•			
a	a	a	a	ab	ab	ab	ab	ab	ab	a	a
•	•	•	•	•	•	•	•	•	•	•	•
•	•	•	•							•	•
b	b	b	b	bc	ac	ac	ac	ac	ac	b	b
								•	•		
•	•	•	•	•	•	•	•	•	•	•	•
				•	•	•	•	•	•	•	•
				•a	•a	•a	•a	•	•	•	
•	•	•	•	•ab	•ab	•ab	•ab	•a	•a	•	•

For further information on specific sites, contact the BC Environment office in your region. The head office can be reached in Victoria at (604) 387-9767.

BC SANCTUARIES AND WILDLIFE VIEWING AREAS

There are a host of parks, wilderness areas and sanctuaries around the province which are helping to preserve the natural beauty of BC for future generations. These living museums serve as a precious heritage for the benefit, enjoyment and education of resident and tourist alike.

ZOOS, NATURE CENTRES AND MUSEUMS

ABBOTSFORD

Fraser Valley Trout Hatchery
State-of-the-art displays including a living stream.
34345 Vye Rd., Abbotsford
Phone: 852-5388

ALDERGROVE

Vancouver Game Farm
110 species of animals and birds on 48 hectares.
5048 264 St., Aldergrove
Phone: 856-6825

BURNABY

Burnaby Lake Regional Park and Nature House
Nature house, wildlife sanctuary, 8.5 km of trails.
South off Winston St. at Piper Ave.
432-6350

Seymour Demonstration Forest
Forty km of trails through a rich coastal forest, rich diversity of wildlife.
North Vancouver
Phone: 432-6286

CRESTON

Creston Valley Wildlife Management Area
17,000 hectares area is dedicated to wildlife, especially waterfowl. Self-guided trails and an observation tower are present. Seasonal staff offer a variety of programs and eco-tours. Wildlife centre has gift shop and lunch counter.
Phone 428-3260 for directions.

COOMBS

Vancouver Island Butterfly World
Features hundreds of live, free-flying butterflies from around the world.
On highway #4, 1 km west of Coombs.
Phone: 248-7026

COURTENAY

Courtenay Museum
Features a wealth of natural history displays. Significant fossil collection includes the largest specimen of Elasmosaurus, the largest marine reptile found west of the Rockies.
360 Cliffe Ave.
Phone: 334-3611

COWICHAN LAKE

Wildflowers of Honeymoon Bay
Over two dozen species of wildflowers are cultivated, including the world's largest known concentration of pink fawn lilies which bloom each spring.
Honeymoon Bay
Phone: 382-3551

DELTA

George C. Reifel Bird Sanctuary
Over 250 species of birds have been observed on this 340 hectares marshland sanctuary. Migration peaks are February, March, October and November. Gift shop.
5191 Robertson Rd., Delta
Phone: 946-6980

DUNCAN

BC Forest Museum
40 hectare park features numerous exhibits and walking trails. Concession available.
Located north of Duncan on Island Highway.
Phone: 746-1251

Ecomuseum
Ecomuseum is a 1,000 sq. km museum "without walls." Walking tours available.
Phone 746-1611 for directions.

FORT STEELE

Kootenay Trout Hatchery
Provincial trout hatchery features educational displays. Species raised include rainbow, brook and cutthroat trout. Guided tours by appointment.In Fort Steele, 40 km east of Cranbrook.
Phone: 429-3214

KAMLOOPS

Kamloops Wildlife Park
Features 70 species, exhibits, concession and souvenir shop.
9055 East Trans Canada Highway, Kamloops
Phone: 573-3242

LANGLEY

Campbell Valley Regional Park
A valued conservation area featuring a wealth of plants and wildlife. Visitor centre.
South on 200th St. off Highway 1 for 14.5 km east of 16th Ave.
Phone: 530-4983

Derby Reach Regional Park
Four km walking/equestrian trail, group bar fishing sites.
North on 200th St. off Highway 1 to 96th Ave., east to 208th St, north to Allard Cr., east for 3 km.
Phone: 530-4983

MAPLE RIDGE

Kanaka Creek Regional Park
A diverse creek corridor featuring salmon hatchery, waterfalls, wetlands and rich wildlife.
North on 228th St. off Lougheed Hwy to 256th St., turn right and follow signs to hatchery.
Phone: 530-4983

MISSION

Cascade Falls Regional Park
Main feature is series of waterfalls on Cascade Creek.
North on Sylvester Rd. off Highway 7 for 16 km, right on Ridgeway Dr.
Phone: 826-1291

Grant Narrows Regional Park
Nature trails provide opportunities to view migrant birds and wildlife.
Phone 826-1291 for directions.

Neilson Regional Park
Ten hectare park features walking trails and a fish-rearing centre.
8745 East Edwards Road, Mission
Phone: 826-1291

MOUNT ROBSON

Mount Robson Provincial Park Nature House
At Mount Robson Provincial Park.
Phone: 566-4325

NAKUSP

Hill Creek Spawning Channel and Hatchery
Spawning Kokanee return each fall to the 3.2 km long spawning channel. Hatchery raises Rainbow Trout, Dolly Varden and Kokanee.
Galena Bay, 50 km NE of Nakusp on Highway 23.
Phone: 352-6033

NANAIMO

Grant Ainscourt Arboretum
Facility illustrates the behaviour and growth of local and exotic species.
Located 11.3 km south of Nanaimo at junction of Harmac Pulp Mill Road and Duke Point Road.
Phone: 755-3467

Karlin Rose Garden
Features 800 varieties of roses.
At corner of Prideaux St. and Comox St.

Morrell Nature Sanctuary
Sanctuary encompasses 111 hectares of mixed Douglas-Fir, White Pine and Arbutus forests. 11.5 km of walking trails. Guided tours available on request.
1050 Nanaimo Lake Road
Phone: 753-5811

NORTH VANCOUVER

Capilano River Regional Park and Cleveland Dam
Extensive trails wind through a spectacular river canyon.
Take the Grouse Mountain exit north off the Capilano Highway to the Cleveland Dam parking lot.
Phone: 432-6350

Capilano Salmon Hatchery
Displays of salmon life cycles and live adult and juvenile salmon.
4500 Capilano Park Road
Phone: 666-1790

Lynn Canyon Ecology Centre and Suspension Bridge
Displays on the relationships between living creatures; nature trails; suspension bridge.
3663 Park Road, North Vancouver
Phone: 987-5922

OKANAGAN FALLS

Memorial Rose Garden
Features 190 species of hybrid teas.
Highway 97 beside Centennial Park.
Phone: 497-5309

PENTICTON

Okanagan Game Farm
View 125 species of animals from around the world on a 240 hectare refuge. Drive or walk. Lunch counter and gift shop. 8 km south of Penticton on Highway 97.
Phone: 497-5405

PORT ALBERNI

Robertson Creek Fish Hatchery
Hatchery is located in scenic area featuring hiking trails, abundant bird and animal life.
Located in Port Alberni.
Phone: 724-6521

PORT MOODY

Belcarra Regional Park
Extensive network of walking and hiking trails, 9 km of marine shoreline.
Phone 432-6350 for directions.

PORT RENFREW

Botanical Beach
Marine scientists from around the world visit this unique area with abundant and diverse intertidal life. Access road may be washed out, so phone BC Parks before leaving at 387-4363 in Victoria.
Located at end of Cerantes Road.
Phone: 387-4363

QUALICUM BEACH

Qualicum River Salmon Hatchery
Features hatchery, spawning channel, information centre and project model.
Hiking trails nearby.
RR #3
Phone: 757-8412

Good Earth Farm
Features floral and oriental gardens, including a permanent bonsai display.
Five km north of Qualicum Beach
Phone: 752-9332

RICHMOND

Fantasy Gardens
Features three botanical theme gardens.
10800 Number 5 Rd.
Phone: 277-7777

Iona Beach Regional Park
Forty-two km of trails along jetty with panoramic views of the Gulf Islands and North Shore Mountains. Features nesting area for wide variety of birds.
Iona Island, north of Vancouver International Airport.
Phone: 432-6350

Richmond Nature Park
A unique bog environment in which to enjoy native plants, animals and birds. Nature house and guided tours.
11851 Westminster Highway
Phone: 273-7015

SIDNEY

Sidney Marine Mammal and Historical Museum
Features displays on the ecology of whales, sea lions, seals and sea otters. Gift shop.
2538 Beacon Ave.
Phone: 656-1322

SOOKE

East Sooke Park
1,422 hectares sanctuary where the forest meets the sea. Wide diversity of flora and fauna.
Located in east Sooke.
Phone: 478-3344

SUMMERLAND

Summerland Trout Hatchery
View brook char and rainbow trout.
RR #1, Site 11, Lakeshore Dr.
Phone: 494-0491

SURREY

Redwood Park
Main attraction is the largest stand of redwood trees north of California.
20th Ave. and 180th St.
Phone: 591-4418

Tynehead Regional Park
Hike on extensive trails through second-growth forests and meadows. Visit salmon hatchery by appointment.
Phone 530-4983 for directions.

TSAWWASSEN

Boundary Bay Regional Park
Excellent waterfowl and shorebird viewing area, 1.6 km of superb sandy beach.
East on 12th Ave. off 56th St. to Boundary Bay Road
Phone: 432-6350

VANCOUVER

Stanley Park
This famous 400 hectares park located in the heart of the city features a zoo, children's petting zoo and world famous aquarium. The park is latticed by numerous trails and bikepaths. Rich flora and fauna are evident throughout.
Stanley Park
Phone: 681-1146

Pacific Spirit Regional Park
50 km of walking, hiking, cycling and equestrian trails through varied deciduous and coniferous forests, bogs and estuaries. Fifty entrance points surrounding UBC.
Phone: 432-6350

Science World
Four galleries of science exhibits are available for hands-on exploration.
1455 Quebec St.
Phone: 687-7832

Vancouver Aquarium
Home to whales, otters, seals and a myriad of sea life from around the world. Walk-through Amazon forest features free-ranging sloths, monkeys and birds. Gift shop.
Stanley Park
Phone: 685-3364

VICTORIA

Albert Head Lagoon Park
Lagoon serves as a wildlife sanctuary and is an excellent area for birding.
Located in Metchosin off Farhill Road near Albert Head.
Phone: 478-3344

Beacon Hill Park
Beautiful 62 hectares park features wide diversity of plants and animals.
Located between Douglas St. and Cook St.
Phone: 361-0600

Devonian Park
Nature sanctuary features walking trails and excellent bird watching.
In Metchosin, off William Head Road.
Phone: 478-3344

Francis/King Park
Ninety-one hectares park features 11 km of walking trails through Douglas-Fir forest. Nature house and guided tours available.
Located off Prospect Road near Thetis Lake Municipal Park.
Phone: 478-3344

Pacific Undersea Gardens
Natural aquarium features over 5,000 local specimens and the world's only undersea theatre.
490 Belleville St.
Phone: 382-5217

Royal British Columbia Provincial Museum
Museum features award-winning exhibits on the human and natural history of British Columbia. Numerous lectures and special exhibits throughout the year. Tea room and gift shop.
675 Belleville St., Victoria
Phone: 387-3701

Swan Lake Nature Centre
Forty hectares sanctuary located in marsh/lake environment. New nature house features library, display area and classroom. Summer tours and natural history programs are also available.
3873 Swan Lake Road, Victoria
Phone: 479-0211

WILLIAMS LAKE

Scout Island Nature Centre
Nature House has natural history displays. Walking trails wind through marsh, grassland and woods where a variety of flora and fauna can be observed.
Located on Scout Island at the end of Williams Lake.
Phone: 398-8532

BOTANICAL CONSERVATORIES

VAN DUSEN BOTANICAL GARDENS — VANCOUVER

Set on 22 hectares of rolling lawns, Van Dusen Gardens is a year-round blooming showcase of 6,700 species of plants from around the world. With gardens representing a vast array of geographical and botanical regions, Van Dusen is home to Canada's largest collection of rhododendrons and outdoor ornamental plants. Other attractions include a living maze, children's garden, gift shop and restaurant. Guided tours are available.
Phone: 266-7194

UNIVERSITY OF BRITISH COLUMBIA BOTANICAL GARDEN — VANCOUVER

Features over 32 hectares of plants from around the world with a large collection of Pacific Coast/Rocky Mountain species. Special theme gardens feature medicinal plants, foods and Asian plants. Gift shop and plant shop.
6250 Stadium Rd., Vancouver
Phone: 228-3928

BLOEDEL FLORAL CONSERVATORY — VANCOUVER

Five hundred species of plants and healthy populations of free-flying tropical birds and fish contained in large geodesic dome. Plazas, lighted fountain and covered walkways surrounding the conservatory create an idyllic environment in which to enjoy plants throughout the year.
33rd Ave. and Cambie St.
Phone: 872-5513

BUTCHART GARDENS — VICTORIA

Spectacular floral garden features dozens of theme gardens. Special events planned throughout the year. Restaurants, seed and gift shops open all year. Local tours available direct from Vancouver and Victoria. One of North America's greatest floral showpieces.
Located 22 km north of downtown Victoria. Take exit off Highway 17 to Butchart Gardens.
Phone: 652-4422

MINTER GARDENS — CHILLIWACK

Eleven theme gardens are featured on 10.8 hectares. Restaurant, gift shop and garden shop.
Exit at Harrison Hot Springs (#135) off Trans Canada Hwy.
Phone: 794-7191

CONSERVATION ASSOCIATIONS

The following organizations are recommended to readers who wish to become more involved with the conservation of our native plants and animals. For information on the nature societies located in your area, contact the Federation of BC Naturalists.

Federation of BC Naturalists
321-1367 W. Broadway
Vancouver, BC
V6H 4A9
Phone: 737-3057 Fax: 738-7175
Canadian Nature Federation
453 Sussex Drive
Ottawa, Ontario
K1N 6Z4
International Wildlife Coalition — Canada
Box 988
Shelburne, Ontario
L0N 1S0
Nature Conservancy of Canada
794-A Broadview Avenue
Toronto, Ontario
M4K 2P7
Northwest Wildlife Preservation Society
Box 34129, Station D
Vancouver, BC
V6J 4N3
World Wildlife Fund
60 St. Clair Avenue East
Toronto, Ontario
M4T 1N5

CHECKLISTS OF COMMON BC PLANTS AND ANIMALS

KINGDOM PLANTAE

DIVISION PHAEOPHYTA — BROWN ALGAE

- ☐ Rockweed
- ☐ Bull Kelp

DIVISION TRACHEOPHYTA

SUBDIVISION SPERMOPSIDA

CLASS CONIFERAE

FAMILY PINACEAE

- ☐ Whitebark Pine
- ☐ Western White Pine
- ☐ Lodgepole Pine
- ☐ Alpine Larch
- ☐ White Spruce
- ☐ Engelmann Spruce
- ☐ Sitka Spruce
- ☐ Western Hemlock
- ☐ Alpine Fir
- ☐ Douglas Fir

FAMILY CUPRESSACEAE

- ☐ Western Red Cedar
- ☐ Yellow Cedar
- ☐ Common Juniper

FAMILY TAXACEAE

- ☐ Western Yew

CLASS ANGIOSPERMAE

SUBCLASS MONOCOTYLEDONEAE

FAMILY ZOSTERACEAE — EELGRASS

- ☐ Eelgrass

FAMILY TYPHACEAE — CATTAIL

- ☐ Common Cattail

FAMILY LILIACEAE — LILIES

- ☐ Nodding Onion
- ☐ Glacier Lily
- ☐ Tiger Lily
- ☐ Star-flowered

- ☐ Solomon's Seal
- ☐ False Asphodel
- ☐ Death Camas
- ☐ Camas
- ☐ Uniflora
- ☐ Western Trillium
- ☐ Twisted Stalk
- ☐ Indian Hellebore

FAMILY ORCHIDACEAE — ORCHIDS

- ☐ Venus' Slipper
- ☐ Northern Green Bog Orchid
- ☐ Rattlesnake Plantain
- ☐ Wild Lily-of-the-Valley

SUBCLASS DICOTYLEDONEAE

FAMILY SALICACEAE — WILLOWS & ALLIES

- ☐ Black Cottonwood
- ☐ Trembling Aspen
- ☐ Pacific Willow
- ☐ Bebb's Willow
- ☐ Scouler Willow
- ☐ Weeping Willow

FAMILY BETULACEAE — BIRCHES & ALLIES

- ☐ Sitka Alder
- ☐ Mountain Alder
- ☐ Water Birch
- ☐ Paper Birch
- ☐ Beaked Hazelnut

FAMILY URTICACEAE — NETTLES

- ☐ Common Nettle

FAMILY CHENOPODIACEAE — GOOSEFOOTS & ALLIES

- ☐ Lamb's Quarters

FAMILY NYMPHAEACEAE — WATER LILIES

- ☐ Yellow Pond Lily

FAMILY RANUNCULACEAE — CROWFOOTS & ALLIES

- ☐ Red and White Baneberry
- ☐ Western Anemone
- ☐ Buttercup
- ☐ Red Columbine

FAMILY BERBERIDACAE — BEARBERRY

- ☐ Tall Mahonia

FAMILY CRUCIFERAE — MUSTARDS & ALLIES

- ☐ Wild Mustard

FAMILY PARNASSIACEAE — GRASS-OF- PARNASSUS

☐ Grass of Parnassus

FAMILY CRASSULACEAE — STONECROP

☐ Stonecrop

FAMILY SAXIFRAGACEAE — SAXIFRAGE

☐ Saxifrage spp.

☐ Oval-leaf Alumroot

FAMILY GROSSULARIACEAE — CURRANTS

☐ Red-flower Currant

FAMILY HYDRANGEACEAE —HYDRANGEAS

☐ Mock Orange

FAMILY ROSACEAE — ROSE FAMILY

☐ Pacific Crab Apple

☐ Shrubby Cinquefoil

☐ Common Wild Rose

☐ Bitter Cherry

☐ Choke Cherry

☐ Wild Red Raspberry

☐ Saskatoon Serviceberry

☐ Thimbleberry

☐ Salmonberry

☐ Hardhack

☐ Wild Strawberry

☐ Large-leaved Avens

☐ Yellow Dryas

☐ European Mountain Ash

FAMILY GERANIACEAE — GERANIUMS

☐ Sticky Purple Geranium

FAMILY ANACARDIACEAE — SUMAC

☐ Sumac

FAMILY CELASTRACEAE — STAFF-TREE

☐ False Box

FAMILY CRASSULACEAE — HAWTHORNS

☐ Black Hawthorn

FAMILY LEGUMINOSAE — PEAS & ALLIES

☐ White Clover

☐ Yellow Locoweed

☐ Arctic Lupine

FAMILY ACERACEAE — MAPLES

☐ Douglas Maple

FAMILY VIOLACEAE — VIOLETS

☐ Early Blue Violet

☐ Yellow Violet

FAMILY ELAEAGNACEAE — OLEASTER FAMILY

- ☐ Silverberry
- ☐ Canadian Buffaloberry

FAMILY ONAGRACEAE — EVENING PRIMROSE FAMILY

- ☐ Fireweed

FAMILY UMBELLIFERAE — CARROT FAMILY

- ☐ Cow Parsnip

FAMILY ARALIACEAE — GINSENG & ALLIES

- ☐ Sagebrush
- ☐ Kinnikinnick

FAMILY CORNACEAE — DOGWOODS

- ☐ Bunchberry
- ☐ Red Osier Dogwood

FAMILY PYROLACEAE — WINTERGREENS

- ☐ Common Pink Wintergreen

FAMILY MONOTROPACEAE — INDIAN PIPE

- ☐ Indian Pipe

FAMILY ERICACEAE — HEATH

- ☐ Labrador Tea
- ☐ Bog Rosemary
- ☐ Arbutus
- ☐ Swamp Laurel
- ☐ Canada Huckleberry
- ☐ White Moss Heather
- ☐ Red Heather
- ☐ Pipsissewa

FAMILY PRIMULACEAE — PRIMROSES

- ☐ Shooting Star

FAMILY GENTIANACEAE — GENTIANS

- ☐ Northern Gentian

FAMILY MENYANTHACEAE — BUCK-BEAN

- ☐ Buck-bean

FAMILY ASCLEPIADACEAE — MILKWEED

- ☐ Milkweed

FAMILY POLEMONIACEAE — PHLOX FAMILY

- ☐ Phlox
- ☐ Showy Jacob's Ladder

FAMILY HYDROPHYLLACEAE — WATERLEAF & ALLIES

- ☐ Phacelia Linearis

FAMILY BORAGINACEAE — BORAGE FAMILY

- ☐ Alpine Forget-me-not

FAMILY SCROPHULARIACEAE — FIGWORT FAMILY

- ☐ Yellow Toad-flax
- ☐ Indian Paint-brush
- ☐ Elephant's Head
- ☐ Red Monkey Flower
- ☐ Yellow Monkey Flower
- ☐ Bearded Tongue

FAMILY PLANTAGINACEAE — PLANTAINS

- ☐ Common Plantain

FAMILY RUBIACEAE — MADDER FAMILY

- ☐ Northern Bedstraw
- ☐ Wild Red Raspberry

FAMILY CAPRIFOLIACEAE —HONEYSUCKLE FAMILY

- ☐ Low-bush Cranberry
- ☐ Black Twinberry
- ☐ Snowberry
- ☐ Red-berry Elder

FAMILY CAMPANULACEAE — BLUEBELLS

- ☐ Bluebell

FAMILY COMPOSITAE — COMPOSITE FAMILY

- ☐ Arrow-leaved Coltsfoot
- ☐ Common Yarrow
- ☐ Heart-leaved Arnica
- ☐ Common Dandelion
- ☐ Woolly Sunflower
- ☐ Spring Sunflower
- ☐ Pink Pussytoes
- ☐ Canada Thistle
- ☐ Pearly Everlasting
- ☐ Mountain Daisy
- ☐ Cotton Grass
- ☐ Canada Goldenrod
- ☐ Douglas Aster

KINGDOM ANIMALIA

PHYLUM COELENTERATA

- ☐ Sail Jellyfish
- ☐ Brooding Anemone

PHYLUM ANNELIDA — SEGMENTED WORMS

- ☐ Earthworm

PHYLUM MOLLUSCA

- ☐ Striped Snail
- ☐ Common Snail
- ☐ Banana Slug
- ☐ Introduced European Slug
- ☐ Whitecap Limpet
- ☐ Native Littleneck Clam
- ☐ Blue Mussel
- ☐ Pacific Oyster
- ☐ Pink Scallop

PHYLUM ARTHROPODA

- ☐ Acorn Barnacle
- ☐ Purple Shore Crab
- ☐ Dungeness Crab

PHYLUM ECHINODERMATA

- ☐ Purple Sea Star
- ☐ Giant Spined Sea Star
- ☐ Green Sea Urchin
- ☐ Sand Dollar

PHYLUM CHORDATA

SUBPHYLUM VERTEBRATA

CLASS OSTEICHTHYES — BONY FISHES

ORDER PETROMYZONTIFORMES

FAMILY PETROMYZONTIDAE — LAMPREYS

- ☐ Pacific Lamprey

ORDER ACIPENSERIFORMES

FAMILY ACIPENSERIDAE — STURGEONS

- ☐ White Sturgeon

ORDER SALMONIFORMES — SALMON, TROUT & ALLIES

FAMILY SALMONIDAE — SALMON & ALLIES

- ☐ Pink Salmon
- ☐ Coho Salmon
- ☐ Chinook Salmon

- ☐ Sockeye Salmon
- ☐ Chum Salmon
- ☐ Rainbow Trout
- ☐ Cutthroat Trout
- ☐ Lake Trout
- ☐ Brook Trout
- ☐ Dolly Varden
- ☐ Lake Whitefish
- ☐ Mountain Whitefish
- ☐ Arctic Grayling

FAMILY OSMERIDAE — SMELTS

- ☐ Eulachon

ORDER CYPRINIFORMES

FAMILY CYPRINIDAE — MINNOWS & ALLIES

- ☐ Lake Chub
- ☐ Common Carp
- ☐ Redside Shiner

FAMILY CATOSTOMIDAE — SUCKERS

- ☐ White Sucker
- ☐ Longnose Sucker

ORDER GADIFORMES

FAMILY GADIDAE — COD

- ☐ Burbot

ORDER GASTEROSTEIFORMES

FAMILY GASTEROSTEIDAE — STICKLEBACKS

- ☐ Three Spine Stickleback

ORDER PERCIFORMES

FAMILY CENTRARCHIDAE — SUNFISH

- ☐ Pumpkinseed

CLASS AMPHIBIA — AMPHIBIANS

ORDER CAUDATA

FAMILY SALAMANDRIDAE —NEWTS

- ☐ Rough-skinned Newt

FAMILY AMBYSTOMATIDAE — MOLE SALAMANDERS

- ☐ Northwestern Salamander
- ☐ Long-toed Salamander

ORDER ANURA

FAMILY BUFONIDAE —TRUE TOADS

- ☐ Western Toad

FAMILY HYLIDAE — TREE AND GRASS FROGS

- ☐ Pacific Treefrog

FAMILY RANIDAE — TRUE FROGS

- ☐ Red-legged Frog

- ☐ Spotted frog
- ☐ Wood Frog

CLASS REPTILIA — REPTILES

ORDER TESTUDINES

FAMILY EMYDIDAE — FRESHWATER & BOX TURTLES

- ☐ Painted Turtle

ORDER SQUAMATA

FAMILY SCINCIDAE — SKINKS

- ☐ Western Skink

FAMILY ANGUIDAE — ANGUIDS

- ☐ Northern Alligator Lizard

FAMILY COLUBRIDAE — HARMLESS SNAKES

- ☐ Common Garter Snake
- ☐ Northwestern Garter Snake
- ☐ Wandering Garter Snake
- ☐ Gopher Snake

FAMILY VIPERIDAE — PIT VIPERS

- ☐ Prairie Rattlesnake

CLASS AVES

ORDER GAVIIFORMES

FAMILY GAVIIDAE — LOONS

- ☐ Common Loon

ORDER PODICIPEDIFORMES

FAMILY PODICIPEDIDAE — GREBES

- ☐ Red-necked Grebe
- ☐ Western Grebe

ORDER CICONIIFORMES

FAMILY ARDEIDAE — HERONS AND BITTERNS

- ☐ Great Blue Heron

ORDER PELCANIFORMES

FAMILY PHALACROCORACIDAE — CORMORANTS

- ☐ Pelagic Cormorant

ORDER ANSERIFORMES — WATERFOWL

FAMILY ANATIDAE — GEESE, DUCKS & ALLIES

SUBFAMILY CYGNINAE — SWANS

- ☐ Trumpeter Swan

SUBFAMILY ANSERINAE — GEESE

- ☐ Canada Goose
- ☐ Snow Goose

SUBFAMILY ANATINAE — SURFACE-FEEDING DUCKS

- ☐ Mallard
- ☐ Blue-winged Teal

- [ ] Green-winged Teal
- [ ] American Widgeon
- [ ] Northern Shoveler
- [ ] Northern Pintail

SUBFAMILY AYTHYINAE — BAY AND SEA DUCKS

- [ ] Common Goldeneye
- [ ] Bufflehead
- [ ] Harlequin Duck
- [ ] White-winged Scoter

SUBFAMILY MERGINAE — MERGANSERS

- [ ] Common Merganser

SUBFAMILY OXYURINAE — STIFF-TAILED DUCKS

- [ ] Ruddy Duck

ORDER FALCONIFORMES — VULTURES, HAWKS & FALCONS

FAMILY ACCIPITRIDAE — KITES, HAWKS & EAGLES

- [ ] Red-tailed Hawk
- [ ] Bald Eagle
- [ ] Northern Harrier

FAMILY FALCONIDAE — FALCONS

- [ ] American Kestrel

FAMILY PANDIONIDAE

- [ ] Osprey

ORDER GALLIFORMES — CHICKEN-LIKE BIRDS

FAMILY PHASIANIDAE — QUAIL, PARTRIDGES, PHEASANTS & GROUSE

- [ ] Ruffed Grouse
- [ ] Blue Grouse
- [ ] Ring-necked Pheasant
- [ ] White-tailed Ptarmigan

ORDER GRUIFORMES

FAMILY RALLIDAE — COOTS & RAILS

- [ ] American Coot

ORDER CHARADRIIFORMES — SHOREBIRDS, GULLS & ALLIES

FAMILY CHARADRIIDAE — PLOVERS

- [ ] Killdeer

FAMILY SCOLOPACIDAE — SANDPIPERS & PHALAROPES

SUBFAMILY SCOLOPACINAE—SANDPIPERS

- [ ] Common Snipe
- [ ] Spotted Sandpiper
- [ ] Greater Yellowlegs
- [ ] Lesser Yellowlegs

- [ ] Long-billed Dowitcher

FAMILY LARIDAE — GULLS

- [ ] Bonaparte's Gull
- [ ] Glaucous-winged Gull
- [ ] Herring Gull

ORDER COLUMBIFORMES

FAMILY COLUMBIDAE — PIGEONS & DOVES

- [ ] Rock Dove

ORDER STRIGIFORMES

FAMILY STRIGIDAE — OWLS

- [ ] Northern Saw-Whet Owl
- [ ] Great Horned Owl

ORDER CAPRIMULGIFORMES

FAMILY CAPRIMULGIDAE — GOATSUCKERS

- [ ] Common Nighthawk

ORDER APODIFORMES

FAMILY TROCHILIDAE — HUMMINGBIRDS

- [ ] Calliope Hummingbird
- [ ] Rufous Hummingbird

ORDER CORACIIFORMES

FAMILY ALCEDINIDAE — KINGFISHERS

- [ ] Belted Kingfisher

ORDER PICIFORMES

FAMILY PICIDAE — WOODPECKERS

- [ ] Northern Flicker
- [ ] Downy Woodpecker
- [ ] Hairy Woodpecker
- [ ] Yellow-bellied Sapsucker

ORDER PASSERIFORMES — PERCHING BIRDS

FAMILY TYRANNIDAE — FLYCATCHERS

- [ ] Eastern Kingbird
- [ ] Say's Phoebe
- [ ] Olive-sided Flycatcher

FAMILY HIRUNDIDNIDAE — SWALLOWS

- [ ] Tree Swallow
- [ ] Barn Swallow
- [ ] Cliff Swallow

FAMILY CORVIDAE — CROWS & ALLIES

- [ ] Gray Jay
- [ ] Stellar's Jay
- [ ] American Crow
- [ ] Common Raven
- [ ] Black-billed Magpie

FAMILY PARIDAE — CHICKADEES

- [ ] Black-capped Chickadee

☐ Boreal Chickadee

FAMILY SITTIDAE — NUTHATCHES

☐ Red-breasted Nuthatch

FAMILY TROGLODYTIDAE — WRENS

☐ House Wren

FAMILY MUSCICAPIDAE — KINGLETS, THRUSHES & ALLIES

SUBFAMILY SYLVIINAE — KINGLETS

☐ Ruby-crowned Kinglet

SUBFAMILY TURDINAE — THRUSHES & BLUEBIRDS

☐ American Robin
☐ Varied Thrush
☐ Mountain Bluebird

FAMILY BOMBYCILLIDAE — WAXWINGS

☐ Cedar Waxwing
☐ Bohemian Waxwing

FAMILY STURNIDAE — STARLINGS

☐ European Starling

FAMILY VIREONIDAE — VIREOS

☐ Red-eyed Vireo

FAMILY PASSERIDAE — OLD WORLD FINCHES

☐ House Sparrow

FAMILY EMBERIZIDAE — WOOD WARBLERS, SPARROWS, BLACKBIRDS, MEADOWLARKS & ORIOLES

SUBFAMILY PARULINAE — WOOD WARBLERS

☐ Yellow Warbler
☐ Northern Waterthrush
☐ Orange-crowned Warbler
☐ Yellow-rumped Warbler
☐ American Redstart

SUBFAMILY EMBERIZINAE — SPARROWS

☐ Dark-eyed Junco
☐ Fox Sparrow
☐ Chipping Sparrow
☐ Song Sparrow

SUBFAMILY ICTERINAE — BLACKBIRDS & ALLIES

☐ Western Meadowlark
☐ Red-winged Blackbird
☐ Brewer's Blackbird
☐ Brown-headed Cowbird

FAMILY THRAUPIDAE — TANAGERS

☐ Western Tanager

FAMILY FRINGILLIDAE — FINCHES

☐ Pine Siskin

- ☐ American Goldfinch
- ☐ Red Crossbill
- ☐ Evening Grosbeak

CLASS MAMMALIA — MAMMALS

ORDER MARSUPIALIA — OPOSSUMS

- ☐ Opossum

ORDER INSECTIVORA — INSECTIVORES

FAMILY SORICIDAE — SHREWS

- ☐ Masked Shrew
- ☐ Coast Mole

ORDER CHIROPTERA — BATS

FAMILY VESPERTILIONIDAE — PLAINNOSE BATS

- ☐ Little Brown Bat
- ☐ Big Brown Bat

ORDER LAGOMORPHA — RABBIT-LIKE MAMMALS

FAMILY OCHOTONIDAE — PIKAS

- ☐ Rocky Mountain Pika

FAMILY LEPORIDAE — HARES AND RABBITS

- ☐ Nuttall's Cottontail
- ☐ Snowshoe Hare

ORDER RODENTIA — RODENTS

FAMILY SCIURIDAE — SQUIRRELS

- ☐ Yellow Pine Chipmunk
- ☐ Hoary Marmot
- ☐ Columbian Ground Squirrel
- ☐ Golden-mantled Ground Squirrel
- ☐ Red Squirrel
- ☐ Northern Flying Squirrel

FAMILY CASTORIDAE — BEAVER

- ☐ Beaver

FAMILY MURIDAE — MICE, RATS & VOLES

- ☐ Deer Mouse
- ☐ Bushy-tailed Woodrat
- ☐ Southern Boreal Red-backed Vole
- ☐ Bog Lemming
- ☐ Muskrat
- ☐ House Mouse
- ☐ Norway Rat

FAMILY DIPODIDAE — JUMPING MICE

- ☐ Western Jumping Mouse

FAMILY ERETHIZONTIDAE — PORCUPINE

- ☐ Porcupine

ORDER CARNIVORA — CARNIVORES

FAMILY CANIDAE — DOGS

- ☐ Coyote
- ☐ Gray Wolf
- ☐ Red Fox

FAMILY URSIDAE — BEARS

- ☐ Black Bear
- ☐ Grizzly Bear

FAMILY PROCYONIDAE — RACCOONS & ALLIES

- ☐ Raccoon

FAMILY MUSTELIDAE — WEASELS & ALLIES

- ☐ Ermine
- ☐ Mink
- ☐ Badger
- ☐ Striped Skunk
- ☐ Marten
- ☐ River Otter

FAMILY OTARIIDAE — SEA LIONS

- ☐ Northern Sea Lion

FAMILY FELIDAE — CATS

- ☐ Mountain Lion
- ☐ Canada Lynx

ORDER ARTIODACTYLA — CLOVEN-HOOFED MAMMALS

FAMILY CERVIDAE — DEER

- ☐ Elk
- ☐ Mule Deer
- ☐ White-tailed Deer
- ☐ Moose
- ☐ Caribou

FAMILY BOVIDAE — BISON & ALLIES

- ☐ Mountain Goat
- ☐ Bighorn Sheep
- ☐ Dall Sheep

ORDER CETACEA — WHALES, DOLPHINS AND PORPOISES

FAMILY DEPHINIDAE — DOLPHINS AND PORPOISES

- ☐ Pacific White-sided Dolphin
- ☐ Dall's Porpoise
- ☐ Killer Whale

FAMILY ESCHRICHTIIDAE — GRAY WHALE

- ☐ Gray Whale

FAMILY BALAENOPTERIDAE — BALEEN WHALES

- ☐ Humpback Whale

GLOSSARY

Alternate — spaced singly along the stem.

Anther — the part of the stamen that produces pollen.

Albino — an animal lacking external pigmentation.

Annual — a plant which completes its life cycle in one year.

Anterior — pertaining to the front end.

Aquatic — living in water.

Ascending — rising or curving upward.

Barbel — an organ near the mouth of fish used as an organ of taste, touch, or smell.

Berry — a fruit formed from a single ovary which is fleshy or pulpy and contains one or many seeds.

Bloom — a whitish powdery or waxy covering.

Bract — a scale or leaf, usually small.

Branchlet — a twig from which leaves grow.

Boss — a rounded knob between the eyes of some toads.

Burrow — a tunnel excavated and inhabited by an animal.

Carnivorous — feeding primarily on meat.

Cold-blooded — refers to animals which are unable to regulate their own body temperature. This designation is considered inappropriate by many since "cold-blooded" species are capable of maintaining temperatures as high, or higher, than endotherms on warm days.

Compound Leaf — a leaf divided into two or more leaf-like parts (leaflets).

Deciduous — shedding annually.

Diurnal — active primarily during the day.

Dorsal — pertaining to the back or upper surface.

Ecology — the study of the relationships between organisms, and between organisms and their environment.

Ectotherm — animals which regulate their body temperature behaviourally from outside sources of heat, e.g., the sun.

Endotherm — an animal which regulates its body temperature internally.

Flower stalk — the stem bearing the flowers.

Fruit — the matured, seed-bearing ovary.

Habitat — the physical area in which organisms live.

Herbivorous — feeding primarily on vegetation.

Insectivorous — feeding primarily on insects.

Invertebrate — animals lacking backbones, e.g., worms, slugs, crayfish, shrimps.

Lance-shaped — a leaf which is much longer than it is broad, widest near its base and tapered at the tip.

Larva — immature forms of an animal which differ from the adult.

Lateral — located away from the mid line, at or near the sides.

Lobe — a projecting part of a leaf or flower, usually rounded.

Nest — a structure built for shelter or insulation.

Nocturnal — active primarily at night.

Omnivorous — feeding on both animal and vegetable food.

Ovary — the female sex organ which is the site of egg production and maturation.

Perennial — a plant that lives for several years.

Petal — the coloured outer parts of a flower head.

Piscivorous — feeding primarily on fish.

Pistil — the central organ of the flower which develops into a fruit.

Pollen — tiny grains produced in the anthers which contain the male reproductive cells.

Posterior — pertaining to the rear.

Sepal — the outer, usually green, leaf-like structures that protect the flower bud and are located at the base of an open flower.

Species — a group of interbreeding organisms which are reproductively isolated from other groups.

Spur — a pointed projection.

Subspecies — a relatively uniform, distinct portion of a species population.

Ungulate — an animal that has hooves.

Ventral — pertaining to the under or lower surface.

Verterbrate — an animal possessing a backbone.

Warm-blooded — an animal which regulates its blood temperature internally. "Endotherm" is the preferred designation for this characteristic.

Whorl — a circle of leaves or flowers about a stem.

Woolly — bearing long or matted hairs.

REFERENCES

FLORA

Brockman, C.F. *Trees of North America*. Golden Press, New York, N.Y., 1979.

Clark, L.J. *Wildflowers of the Pacific Northwest*. Gray's Publishing, Sidney, B.C., 1976.

Elias, T.S. *Trees of North America*. Van Rostrand Reinhold Co., New York, N.Y., 1980.

Hosie, R.C. *Native Trees of Canada*. Fitzhenry and Whiteside, Don Mills, Ont., 1979.

Lyons, C.P. *Trees, Shrubs and Flowers to Know in British Columbia*. Evergreen Press Ltd., Vancouver, B.C., 1965.

MacKinnon, A. et al. *Plants of Northern British Columbia*. Lone Pine Publishing, Edmonton, Alta., 1992.

Mitchell, Alan, and More, D. *Trees*. Gallery Books, New York, N.Y., 1990.

Pesman, M.W. *Meet the Natives. A Beginner's Field Guide to Rocky Mountain Wild Flowers, Trees and Shrubs*. Pruett Publishers, Denver, Col., 1988.

Porsild, A.E. *Rocky Mountain Wildflowers*. National Museums of Canada, Ottawa, Ont., 1984.

Spellenberg, R. *The Audubon Society Field Guide to North American Wildflowers*. A. Knopf, New York, N.Y., 1979.

Venning, D. *Wildflowers of North America*. Golden Press, New York, N.Y., 1984.

MAMMALS

Banfield, A.W. *The Mammals of Canada*. University of Toronto Press, Toronto, Ont., 1987.

Burt, W.H., and Grossenheider, R.P. *A Field Guide to the Mammals of America North of Mexico*. Houghton Mifflin, Boston, Mass., 1976.

Walker, E.P. *Mammals of the World*. Johns Hopkins University Press, Baltimore, Md., 1975.

Whitaker, J.D. *The Audubon Society Field Guide to North American Mammals*. A. Knopf, New York, N.Y., 1980.

Wooding, F.H. *Wild Mammals of Canada*. McGraw Hill Ryerson, Toronto, Ont., 1982.

Wrigley, R.E. *Mammals in North America*. Hyperion Press, Winnipeg, Man., 1986.

BIRDS

Godfrey, W.E. *The Birds of Canada*. Queen's Printer, Ottawa, Ont., 1986.

May, C.P. *A Book of Canadian Birds*. MacMillan of Canada, Toronto, Ont., 1967.

Miklos, D.F. *The Audubon Society Field Guide to North American Birds*. A. Knopf, New York, N.Y., 1977.

Peterson, R.T. *A Field Guide to the Western Birds*. Houghton Mifflin Co., Boston, Mass., 1961.

Taverner, P.A. *Birds of Canada*. National Museums of Canada, Ottawa, Ont., 1934.

REPTILES AND AMPHIBIANS

Behler, J.L., and King, F.W. *The Audubon Society Field Guide to North American Reptiles and Amphibians.* A. Knopf, New York, N.Y., 1979.

Cook, F. *Introduction to Canadian Amphibians and Reptiles.* National Museums of Canada, Ottawa, Ont., 1984.

Froom, B. *Snakes of Canada.* McClelland and Stewart, Toronto, Ont., 1972.

Stebbins, R.C. *Amphibians and Reptiles of Western North America.* Houghton Mifflin Co., Boston, Mass., 1985.

Smith, H., and Brodie, E. *Reptiles of North America.* Golden Press, New York, N.Y., 1982.

Zim, H.S., and Smith, H.M. *Reptiles and Amphibians. A Guide to Familiar American Species.* Golden Press, New York, N.Y., 1956.

FISH

McAllister, D.E., and Crossman, E.J. *A Guide to the Freshwater Sport Fishes of Canada.* National Museums of Canada, Ottawa, Ont., 1973.

Thompson, Peter. *Thompson's Guide to Freshwater Fishes.* Houghton Mifflin Co., Boston, Mass., 1985.

Zim, H.S. *Fishes: A Guide to Familiar American Species.* Simon and Schuster, New York, N.Y., 1956.

INVERTEBRATES

Abbott, R.T. *Seashells of North America.* Golden Press, New York, N.Y., 1968.

Harbo, Rick, M. *Guide to the Western Seashore.* Hancock House, Surrey, B.C., 1988.

Rehder, H.A. *The Audubon Society Field Guide to North American Seashells.* A. Knopf, New York, N.Y., 1981.

Zim, H. *Seashores, A Guide to Animals and Plants Along the Beaches.* Golden Press, New York, N.Y., 1964.

ECOLOGY

Ford, J.M., and Monroe, J.M. *Living Systems, Principles and Relationships.* Canfield Press, San Franciso, Calif., 1977.

Franke, R.G. *Man and the Changing Environment.* Holt, Rinehart and Winston, Toronto, Ont., 1975.

Keeton, W.T. *Biological Science.* Norton and Company, New York, N.Y., 1980.

Lawrence, R.D. *The Natural History of Canada.* Key Porter, Toronto, Ont., 1988.

Livingston, J., and Fitzharris, T. *Canada, A Natural History.* Viking Studio Books, Markham, Ont., 1988.

Ransom, J.E. *Harper and Row's Complete Field Guide to North American Wildlife, Western Edition.* Harper and Row, New York, N.Y., 1981.

Whitney, S. *A Sierra Club Naturalist's Guide to the Pacific Northwest.* Sierra Club Books, San Francisco, Calif., 1989.

Index

C

D

E

F

G

H

N

O

P

Y

Z

ABOUT THE AUTHOR

Jim Kavanagh is a writer and naturalist living in Vancouver with his wife, Jill and daughter, Kristen. His previous book, *Nature Alberta*, is a Canadian bestseller.